W9-BMU-429

9/03

92 Rem

Foundation
51 grant

υ αι.00

artists would be judged. In a lifetime of painting and sculpting, he created a visual record of the colorful frontier years that would never be equaled.

His life was like a shooting star, short in duration but brilliant. He worked at a dizzying pace, producing twenty-two sculptures and nearly three thousand drawings and paintings. Most of these bristle with action. They capture the wild, dangerous days when cavalry and American Indians fought to the death and cowboys struggled to control stampeding cattle. In his later years Remington turned to quieter things—stagecoaches in the moonlight, and American Indians keeping silent watch under the stars.

Custer's Last Stand

Growing up in New York State, Remington was fascinated by the West long before he saw it. He listened to stories about the great waves of settlers who headed for the territories in covered wagons before the Civil War. He was a teenager in 1876 when he heard the news that shocked the nation: On June 25, General George Armstrong Custer and his men had been wiped out by Sioux and Cheyenne warriors at Montana's Little Bighorn River.

President Ulysses S. Grant, ignoring an important treaty, had sent the Seventh Cavalry to force American Indians not yet on reservations to surrender. Vowing never to do so, Sioux leaders Sitting Bull and Crazy Horse organized the largest fighting force of their people ever seen. The warriors turned Custer's surprise attack into a deathtrap and surrounded the cavalry, "swirling like water round a stone," according to one Cheyenne warrior.[2] "Custer's Last Stand," as the Battle of the Little Bighorn is sometimes called, was a humiliating defeat for the United States Army. For the Plains Indians it was the last great victory.

First Taste of the West

Five years after the Battle of the Little Bighorn, when he was nineteen, Remington went West for the first time. He was just in time to see the last years of the frontier, where white and native civilizations met and clashed. By 1881 the Indian Wars were all but over. Towns and telegraph poles marked the prairie, signs that the United States was quickly fulfilling its "Manifest Destiny," its plan to settle the land from the Atlantic to the Pacific Ocean.

After he became famous, Remington wrote that it was on this first trip that he decided to become a painter of the American West. To record the "grand silent country" in pictures was the only way to preserve the old days, he thought. "I knew the wild riders and the vacant land were about to vanish forever, and the more I considered the subject the bigger Forever loomed."[3]

2

A BOY FROM THE NORTH COUNTRY

In New York State, high up near the Canadian border, is a little town called Canton. It is nestled between the Adirondack Mountains and the St. Lawrence River, where summers are short and winter comes early, muffled in snow. Here in the North Country, the short, amazing life of Frederic Sackrider Remington began.

A Quiet Town in an Unquiet Time

Frederic Remington was born on October 4, 1861, in his grandparents' tidy wooden house and was welcomed by all the aunts, uncles, and cousins who lived nearby. The Remingtons were an important family in town. Grandfather Seth Williston

Remington was a pastor and a founder of St. Lawrence University. The family of Frederic's mother, Clara Sackrider Remington, owned a thriving hardware business. And his father, Seth Pierre Remington, published the *St. Lawrence Plaindealer*, Canton's only newspaper. It was a comfortable place to grow up, where people traveled by horse and buggy and everyone knew everyone else.

But Canton was a quiet town in an unquiet time. The Civil War had begun just six months before Frederic's birth. His father, Seth, was intensely patriotic for the Union— the Northern states—and a strong supporter of President Abraham Lincoln and the Republican Party. When Fred was only two months old, Seth decided to join the bitter fight to end slavery. He enlisted in the Eleventh New York Cavalry. After selling his newspaper, he kissed his wife and baby good-bye and went to war.

"The Colonel"

Captain Seth Pierre Remington soon earned the wartime rank of colonel and distinguished himself for bravery. He could lead a thundering cavalry charge into enemy ranks, with gun or flashing saber in hand. On one occasion he refused to surrender to Confederate troops that had surrounded him. (The Confederate states were those in the South that were trying to separate from the United States.) In spite of the cannonballs tearing through the air, he led his men out of the trap. For his fearlessness he would long be remembered by his soldiers.[1]

At the war's end Seth came home to a joyous hero's welcome. Now known by everyone as "the Colonel," he repurchased his newspaper and settled down to write political editorials and to get to know his much loved and only child.

Father and Son

Everyone looked up to the likable Colonel, but no one more than Fred. The little boy did not have to imagine what a war hero was like—a real one lived in his home. Listening to his father's stories about the bold, galloping cavalry, he fell in love with the military with an intensity that would last all his life and guide his entire career in art. Seth Remington thought of his son as "my dear little Fred." When Fred was a teenager, he would affectionately call his father "the old boy."

Although he worshiped "the old boy," young Remington was no perfect model of behavior himself. Stocky, blond, and a mischievous tease, he was a natural athlete and a natural ringleader. With his band of friends, he was always running somewhere, hoping to escape his mother's clutches. In the summer the children fished, canoed, and swam. When winter came, they skated on homemade skates and raced downhill on their sleds. Fred lived to be outdoors in the countryside and, naturally, hated being cooped up in school.

One August night in 1869, he awoke to frantic shouts of "Fire! Fire!" Canton's main business street was going up in flames. The only firefighting tools the townspeople owned were buckets, which were filled with water and passed hand-to-hand in a long line from the river. Eight-year-old Fred joined the bucket line, but the fire raged out of control. Many businesses, including the printing plant for his father's newspaper, were reduced to ashes.

The Colonel reestablished his paper up the street. And taking charge as usual, he helped organize the St. Lawrence Fire Department, complete with a machine for pumping water by hand. Less than one year later, another devastating fire broke out. But to everyone's surprise, the new machine's hose proved too short to reach the burning buildings. There was nothing for the people of Canton to do but rebuild once again.

This time Seth Remington arranged for the purchase of impressive, up-to-date hook-and-ladder equipment and created Engine Company Number One. In 1872, ten-year-old Fred felt like a hero himself when he became the "official mascot" of the company. Dressed in a pint-sized uniform, he posed for a solemn photograph with the real firefighters.

Young Frederic sits with his mother, Clara Sackrider Remington.

He was also allowed to lead the men as they marched in Canton's grand Fourth of July parade.

Riding and Sketching Horses

In 1873, Seth sold his paper for the last time and moved his family to nearby Ogdensburg, where he took the desirable job of customs collector. But he was still a cavalryman at heart; his real love in life was horses. With a partner, Walter Van Valkenburg (known as "Van"), he found time to start a business training and selling horses for trotting races.

Fred spent every possible minute at his father's stables. No place in the world seemed as wonderful to him. His father and Van taught him the fine points of grooming and judging a horse and took him to county fairs to watch the races. Fred became an expert rider and even learned to drive a two-wheeled racing cart called a sulky. By now Fred's nickname was Puffy, probably because he had inherited his mother's big-boned frame and tendency to put on weight. But this did not prevent him from becoming an accomplished athlete.

When he was not riding horses, he was sketching them. Fred had started to draw at age two and had never stopped. He doodled on any blank space he could find, whether on scrap paper or in the margins of his schoolbooks. The urge to draw was as strong in Fred as the urge to make mischief. In Ogdensburg

he drew his favorite animals galloping or standing still, from every angle he could think of.

Military School

These perfect boyhood days came to an end in 1875, when Fred's parents sent him to a military school in Vermont. They hoped that he would follow in his father's footsteps and have a distinguished army career. At first, fourteen-year-old Remington was enthusiastic. But soon the strict rules upset him.

Another school, Highland Military Academy in Massachusetts, was an improvement. Fifteen years old now, Fred was better prepared for boarding school life. His favorite academic class was English composition, where he discovered that he had a knack for writing. In a humorous letter to his uncle Robert Sackrider, he wrote, "I am studying real hard now, no fooling. Haint studied so much since I was a boy. . . ."[2]

He eagerly learned military tactics in the "Awkward Squad," where the new cadets started out, and he liked wearing his cadet uniform with its shiny brass buttons. But Remington was too rambunctious to submit for long to the discipline of military training, and he decided that he would never be a professional soldier.

At fifteen, he was about five feet eight inches tall and weighed a hefty 180 pounds. He was extremely popular with the other boys because of his athletic skill and his easygoing ways. If there was fun to be had, Fred would find it. As a teenager he was still dashing off drawings, and these attracted attention, too. In a letter to another boy who loved to draw, Fred wrote, "Your favorite subject is soldiers. So is mine. . . ." He also liked western subjects: "Send me Indians, cowboys, villains or toughs. These are what I want. . . ."[3]

Becoming an Artist

At graduation Fred considered the future. The army was not for him, and a desk job also seemed out of the question. As he told his Uncle Horace, "No sir, I will never burn any mid-night oil in squaring accounts." Hoping to do only what he enjoyed, he thought of combining journalism and art in a career. One thing was certain to him: "I mean to study for an artist anyhow whether I ever make a success of it or not."[4] By now Fred's sketchbooks were overflowing. On the last page of one book, he drew a picture of himself striding toward the western sunset, with a portfolio in one hand and a paintbrush in the other.[5]

No one in the Remington family had ever been an artist, yet Fred's parents allowed him to go to art school. He enrolled in Yale's School of Fine Arts in

1878, just before his seventeenth birthday—as the only male first-year student. The school was run on the European model—students spent the first two years perfecting drawing techniques before attempting to paint in the third year.

In the dim basement studio where classes were held, boisterous Fred Remington felt wildly out of place. How bored he was sitting for hours, sketching plaster replicas of ancient Greek statues. To help pass the time, he struck up a friendship with one of the few young men in the art school, a fourth-year student named Poultney Bigelow. But it was not enough to drive away the gloomy mood in the basement, and it was probably at Yale that Fred developed a permanent dislike for the academic side of art.

Boxing and Football

College life outside of art class was exciting, though. Remington, once described as "a bull for size and strength," boxed for the university.[6] He also played on the varsity football team, sharing the glory as Yale won game after game. He thrived on the crashing danger of the sport. A story has circulated that before one game, Remington dipped his football jersey in blood from a slaughterhouse to "make it look more businesslike."[7] Whether or not this is true, he was certainly not a typical art student.

The first Remington drawing ever to be published appeared in the college newspaper, the *Yale Courant*. It was a comical sketch of a football player with a bandaged leg. The title was *Campus Riff-Raff*; the caption read "Good gracious, old fellow, what have you been doing with yourself?"[8]

Falling in Love

The fun-loving, football-playing art student went home for the summer in 1879. There he fell in love—for the first time and forever—with Eva Caten, of Gloversville, New York. Eva, whose nickname was Missie, was a student at St. Lawrence University, the college that Remington's grandfather had helped to found. Two years older than Fred, she was small and lively, with blue eyes and brown, wavy hair. At summer's end, the

Frederic Remington poses in his Yale football uniform.

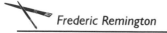

young couple had to separate, but their feelings for each other remained strong.

Saying Goodbye to the Colonel

At Christmas, Frederic Remington faced grief. Seth Remington had been struggling with tuberculosis, and his son's hopes that good food and exercise would jolt "the old boy" back to health came to nothing. Seth died at age forty-six, on February 18, 1880. The local newspaper praised his heroism during the Civil War and his "calm, brave, honest life."[9]

Remington's life would never be the same. He had lost his "Venerable Papa," the man he most admired and loved. Remington was only eighteen when his father died.

Mother and son moved from Ogdensburg back to Canton to be with the family. Since art school had seemed so stale to him, Remington decided not to return to Yale. In spite of his earlier decisions to combine journalism and art and never to work behind a desk, he now had to be practical. He needed a job.

Remington's uncle Mart, who was a politician in Albany, found him work in the Albany office of the governor of New York. Remington tried to play the role his family had cast him in—promising young Republican professional. But he grew restless doing dull paperwork and quit to work for a city newspaper. Then followed two more jobs that he disliked, until he had quit four in just one year. People back home began to wonder if the Colonel's energetic son was turning into a "do-nothing."

This lack of stability also worried his sweetheart Eva's father, Lawton Caten. From Albany, Remington wrote to Mr. Caten, asking for permission to marry Eva. The answer was a firm no.

Unable to marry the woman he loved and unwilling to settle down to an ordinary profession, Remington was floundering. Yet his mother frowned on art as much too risky for a career. So, still trying to please her, Remington agreed to try a fifth job in Albany. But first he would treat himself to a trip out West—that strange land that he had dreamed about ever since he had first heard the word *cowboy*.

Montana, the Big Sky Country

After a long journey by train, stagecoach, and horseback, Remington reached the territory of Montana. At the windswept place where Custer had fallen, he saw the graves of the dead soldiers.

Remington continued to explore. So much was different now, in 1881, but much of what he saw was still like the Wild West he had read about in books. He met fur trappers, hunters, and drifters who followed the edge of the frontier as it moved

The Army's Revenge

Immediately after the Battle of the Little Bighorn, Colonel Nelson Miles (whom the American Indians called Bear Coat) led the army in its quest for revenge. In the frozen dead of winter, the soldiers pursued the small bands of free Sioux and Cheyenne, killing their ponies and burning their food supplies. Little by little the people of the Plains had surrendered. In 1877 Crazy Horse was killed. And only weeks before Remington's trip, the great Sitting Bull had finally given up, saying: "I wish it to be remembered that I was the last man of my tribe to surrender my rifle."[10]

ever westward. He encountered cowboys with six-shooters on their hips and gold miners out to strike it rich. He spoke to cavalrymen and saw American Indians riding spotted ponies over the land they had so recently lost.

One evening he shared the campfire of an old man who had been a wagon freighter all his life, hauling supplies throughout the West. As coffee brewed and bacon fried, the stranger told stories of the old days. Then to Remington's dismay, he complained bitterly, ". . . there is no more West."[11] The first transcontinental railroad, which had connected both sides of the continent since 1869, was quickly putting the old-timer out of a job.

And as train tracks fanned out over the prairie, so did the population. People came from the East to start farms and build towns. Some came to hunt the buffalo. Millions of the shaggy creatures had once darkened the plains, but by the time of Remington's trip, hunters had killed all but a few thousand. Great piles of their white bones littered the land.

With his sharp eye and quick pencil, Frederic Remington tried to take in everything he saw. One day he would write, "Without knowing exactly how to do it, I began to try to record some facts around me, and the more I looked the more the panorama unfolded."[12] He even sent a rough sketch of cowboys to *Harper's Weekly* magazine in New York.

Moving to the Kansas Plains

Back in Albany all Remington could think about was the West—especially when his cowboy drawing was actually published. Upon turning twenty-one, Remington received a nine-thousand-dollar inheritance from his father's estate. Now he was free to create a life more to his liking. So with part of the money, he bought a sheep ranch in Kansas, next to one owned by a friend from Yale named Robert Camp. Maybe he could make his fortune there, he thought, and still have plenty of time for art. Already he had the feeling that he was to express many years later: "Everything in the West is life."[13]

3

"WESTERN DREAMS"

The sheep ranch was a definite improvement on the streets and offices of Albany. It consisted of a three-room ranch house, two barns, and a corral—a little island in a sea of flat Kansas grassland. Within a few months Remington spent the rest of his inheritance improving the ranch buildings and doubling the size of his property. In addition to sheep he bought horses and mules.

Life on the Ranch

Remington was amazed to discover that ranching was backbreaking work. There would be no easy fortune. His friend, Robert Camp, did not mind the violent Plains weather and the exhausting job of feeding, doctoring, and shearing the sheep. But Remington did. He let his hired hands do the hardest work and gave himself the pleasant task of ranch cook.

As always Remington put much of his boundless energy into having a good time. Attracting the area's rowdiest young men to his ranch, he organized horse races, steer-roping contests, and boxing matches, which he often won. He also loved to go drinking with his friends in the nearby town of Peabody.

But just as in his boyhood, art and horses were his greatest joys. Remington covered the walls of his little house with drawings. He sketched people and horses whenever he could. And he often played hooky from the ranch to go tearing across the prairie on his horse, Terra Cotta.

Chasing jackrabbits on the prairie was the Kansas version of fox hunting, and it was one of Remington's favorite pastimes. He describes the joy of the chase in "Coursing Rabbits on the Plains," his first published article: ". . . the gallop across the prairie . . . was glorious. . . . Terra Cotta's stride was steel springs under me as she swept along, brushing the dew from the grass of the range."[1]

Soon he gave up on ranching altogether. After only ten months on the prairie, he had run out of money and the will to keep the venture going. Never one to publicly admit defeat, Remington returned to Canton, acting cheerful and successful.

The *Plaindealer*, which noted hometown comings and goings, reported, "He is an enthusiastic admirer of Kansas, not as a home, but as a place to make money. He has recently sold out his lands there and appears to have done well."[2]

Going to Kansas City

Undefeated by this latest false start, Remington made a new plan. "Why not start a hardware ranch out West,"[3] he suggested to a friend. And he headed West again, this time to Kansas City, Missouri. It was a town that needed the hardware and railroad supplies that he and his partner, Charles Ashley, planned to sell.

Growing at a fantastic rate, Kansas City was the largest livestock market in the country. New railroad lines brought in cattle and hogs from points West to be slaughtered and shipped back East as meat. Travelers crisscrossing the United States stopped in the city to conduct business or relax. Real estate was booming, with buildings of every kind popping up like mushrooms after a rain. With all this activity it was a wonder that Remington and Ashley's "hardware ranch" failed almost right away.

Once again Remington was at loose ends, but not for a moment did he let this interfere with his having fun. He became a regular at the city's pool halls and saloons, drinking, playing cards, and competing in boxing matches. He mixed easily with everyone from bartenders to cowboys. When he was not swapping stories with his new pals, he was busy penciling their portraits. One pool-hall worker remembered him affectionately as "One Grand Fred."[4]

"One Grand Fred" certainly knew the saloon business from an insider's point of view. He decided to invest the money left from the sale of his ranch in a partnership in a saloon called Bishop & Christie's. It was a "silent partnership," to be kept secret from Eva Caten and other folks back home. There was no chance that they would approve of such a "vulgar" occupation for the Colonel's only son.

Marriage, Poverty, and an Artist's Passion

During a visit to Canton, Remington proposed to Eva a second time. She was twenty-five now, and this time her father did not stand in her way. On October 1, 1884, Fred and Eva were married. The newlyweds settled in Kansas City in a small house that Remington had bought.

The only trouble was that he had told Eva he was still the owner of a hardware business. She had no idea that he was spending his days at Bishop & Christie's sketching and shooting pool. When she found out about her husband's "silent partnership," Eva was shocked. It was bad enough to be the wife of a saloon owner, but to be deceived was even

Frederic Remington and his wife, Eva, are pictured with tennis rackets. This photo was taken around the time of their marriage.

worse. After only three months of marriage, she packed her things and went sadly back to Gloversville to wait for her husband to change his irresponsible ways. But Remington would not and could not follow her; every cent he had was tied up in the saloon.

Then Remington's life really hit bottom. He was swindled out of his investment in Bishop & Christie's. Now all his money was gone. At twenty-four he found himself deserted by his wife and with no ready means of making a living. He had scored a long string of job failures in just a few years. A less determined person might have given up and gone quietly back to his wife and one of those secure jobs in Albany. A less optimistic person might, at this point, have lost confidence in himself.

Instead, Frederic Remington focused on the one bright spot, the constant passion he had had all his life—art. In Kansas City, just as on the sheep ranch, he had been drawing and painting constantly. On short trips to the Southwest, he had begun to paint cowboys, American Indians, and settlers. In 1885, a Kansas City art dealer was able to sell several of the southwestern scenes, one for $250—a very large amount at that time. Remington also sold his second sketch to *Harper's Weekly* magazine. He now had hope for the future.

Art was a waste of time, argued his mother and wife. But after so many setbacks, he finally knew that it was the only profession he wanted, and he decided to pursue it no matter what the cost. His bad luck in Kansas City had turned into a golden opportunity. He later recalled, "Now that I was poor I could gratify my inclination for an artist's career. In art, to be conventional, one must start out penniless."[5]

Riding an Old Mare to Arizona

With Eva back East he had no one to answer to but himself. Legend has it that one day in August 1885, Remington bought a little gray mare for fifty dollars. Early the next morning he rode alone out of Kansas City toward the southwestern territories, looking for more of the western subjects that he loved to paint. A Missouri newspaper published an account of this story many years later, concluding with the following: "They warned him of the perils. He smiled. They coaxed him, but he went. He must have found what he wanted out there, for when his friends next heard of him he was Frederic Remington and people paid real money for his pictures."[6]

Escape of the Apache

But the "real" money was still in the future as Remington made his way on the old mare into the Arizona Territory. (Arizona would not become a state until 1912.) The territory was mostly wild—a land of parched deserts, forbidding mountains, and deep canyons. It was Apache country.

But American cattle ranchers, gold miners, and settlers were also eager to claim the land so they were steadily invading the Apache hunting grounds. The fierce Apache warriors struck back hard. They swooped down on settlements to kill, burn, and steal. Then they would vanish as quickly as they had come, into their mountain strongholds. But they were outnumbered by the white population. And they were eventually overcome by the persistence of the U.S. Army, which paid American Indian scouts to follow the Apache into their remote hiding places.

In 1876 the army forced all the Apache tribes onto one huge reservation in the Arizona Territory. A place of malaria and hunger, it was called San Carlos. The Apache thought of it as the worst place on earth. And there were some who could never

Apache Defenders

The Apache people lived in thatched houses, but moved often to hunt for deer and antelope and to gather wild plants. Roaming the rough terrain mostly on foot, they were ferocious defenders of their turf.

accept it. Geronimo, the most famous warrior of them all, led his small band of Chiricahua Apache in a ten-year struggle against the reservation system. As one Apache fighter said, "All of us knew that we were doomed, but some preferred death to slavery and imprisonment."[7]

In May 1885, shortly before Remington arrived in Arizona, Geronimo had escaped from San Carlos for the third or fourth time, taking with him about one hundred and thirty of his people. They headed for their old shelter in the fortresslike Sierra Madre Mountains in Mexico. From there they could raid settlements on both sides of the border for food and other supplies. Settlers in the neighboring Arizona Territory were filled with dread as they read the newspaper headline: "Apaches Are Out."[8]

Remington filled his sketchbook with pictures of cavalrymen and American Indian scouts—all

of whom were caught up in the drama of Geronimo's escape.

Getting Published

After four weeks in Arizona, Remington returned to Kansas City with a batch of drawings and a longing to see Eva. She missed him too, so they agreed to live together again in New York City. There he would try to get his work published in magazines. He even promised to take another office job if the first scheme failed.

The Remingtons shared a tiny apartment in Brooklyn with another couple. Frederic Remington sent his Arizona drawings to the prestigious *Harper's Weekly*, which had already published two of his sketches. To his amazement, Henry Harper himself, head of the publishing company, asked to meet him.

Remington had a genius for self-promotion. He strode into Harper's office dressed as a cowboy from head to toe. He charmed the publisher with a tall tale or two and gave the impression of being a real westerner "just off a ranch."[9]

By sheer luck Remington's timing was perfect. The news of Geronimo's escape had whetted the public's appetite for on-the-spot information about the defiant Apache. A few old photographs of them were the only images that most easterners had

HARPER'S WEEKLY.

JOURNAL OF CIVILIZATION.

Vol. XXX.—No. 1516.
Copyright, 1886, by Harper & Brothers.

NEW YORK, SATURDAY, JANUARY 9, 1886.

TEN CENTS A COPY
$4.00 PER YEAR, IN ADVANCE.

THE APACHE WAR—INDIAN SCOUTS ON GERONIMO'S TRAIL.—Drawn by Frederic Remington.—[See Page 23.]

The Apache War—Indian Scouts on Geronimo's Trail *appeared on the cover of* Harper's Weekly *on January 9, 1886.*

ever seen. Remington had no sketch of Geronimo himself, but his southwestern drawings captured the harsh flavor of life in the territories. Bold and realistic, they were different in subject matter and style from the work of other illustrators of the day.

Henry Harper called the pictures "very crude," but said that they had "all the ring of new and live material."[10] He published two more drawings in *Harper's*—*The Apaches Are Coming*, and, on the cover, *The Apache War—Indian Scouts on Geronimo's Trail*.

The Art Students League

Remington had to sell many more drawings if he was to support himself and his wife, and he faced tough competition from the many illustrators living in New York. To improve his technique, he enrolled in classes at the Art Students League in March 1886. He was too poor to pay the five dollar monthly tuition, but his uncle Bill Remington, the only family member who thought Fred should become an artist, paid it for him.

At the League, Frederic Remington met other illustrators, such as E. W. Kemble, who would base his career on drawing African Americans, and Charles Dana Gibson, who would become famous as the creator of the "Gibson girl" pictures. Remington took a painting class with the American

Impressionist J. Alden Weir. He worked on his drawing and practiced "ink wash" (a technique similar to watercolor in which a mixture of ink and water is applied to paper with a brush). Fortunately he absorbed a lot in the three-month session, because it would be the last formal art instruction he would ever have. Something much better than art school came along.

In Search of Geronimo

In late spring of 1886, Henry Harper chose Remington to be his correspondent in Arizona, to write and illustrate a series of articles about Geronimo's flight. Remington was to ride along as an eyewitness with General Nelson Miles's cavalry as it pursued the Apache over the desert.

Sensational images in *Harper's Weekly* were sure to bring Remington's work to the attention of the whole country. More than six decades before television, this was the golden age of the newsmagazine. Americans were snapping up these publications for the latest in news stories and pictures. Since photographs were not yet being used to illustrate articles, there was a large market for artists like Remington. Their drawings were copied onto wood engraving blocks and printed along with the stories they depicted.

And *Harper's*, the magazine with the largest circulation of any in the nation, was *the* place to be published. It stayed ahead of the competition by hiring the best writers and artists. (The artist Winslow Homer had illustrated for *Harper's* during the Civil War.) Remington had just been offered the big break of his dreams.

Only a year before, he had ridden southwest out of Kansas City, a failed saloonkeeper with a flair for art. But as is so often true in life, none of his failures had been wasted. In Albany he had learned once and for all that he could never work behind a desk. On the sheep ranch he had soaked up the feeling of prairie life and stored up images of the West that he would later paint. His Kansas City disasters had allowed him to throw everything else aside and commit himself to art.

In June 1886, twenty-four-year-old Remington boarded a train and headed once again for the Arizona Territory. He was no longer an aimless wanderer, but a professional illustrator. As he wrote in his journal (he was a terrible speller!), he was "An Artist in Serch [sic] of Geronimo."[11]

ARTIST OF THE WEST

Frederic Remington never saw Geronimo. A detachment of cavalry was preparing to follow the Apache into Mexico, but the chase promised to be dangerous and long. Would the soldiers even find the Apache, let alone fight them? Harper's needed stories right away, so Remington decided instead to report on the everyday life of the soldiers in the Southwest. What was it like to patrol the territories under the burning sun?

Powhatan Clarke's Buffalo Soldiers

In Tucson, Arizona, Remington met up with the Tenth Cavalry, which was to become his favorite of all the regiments. It was the regiment of African-American

mounted men called buffalo soldiers by the American Indians. Many were ex-slaves; many had fought for the Union in the Civil War.

Their white lieutenant was a young man named Powhatan Clarke. He was to become Remington's closest friend and the recipient of many of his letters, full of jokes and doodles. The lieutenant was everything Remington thought a man should be— brave, reckless, and carefree. Clarke was an outstanding rider. And he was living the rough military life that Remington so admired. "Life is too short to be taken seriously . . .," Clarke would say.[1]

In spite of the 125-degree heat and the stale army biscuits, Remington was glad to be allowed to ride with the Tenth. He wrote about the experience for *Harper's* in a series of illustrated articles called "Soldiering in the Southwest." One sensational picture in the series, *The Rescue of Corporal Scott*, showed Lieutenant Clarke

Remington painted this portrait of his friend Powhatan Clarke.

General Nelson Miles played a key role in the Indian Wars.

saving the life of one of his men during an Apache ambush. Largely because of this publicity, Clarke would receive the Medal of Honor. And as Remington had hoped, it helped his own career, too.

Remington's status as a special correspondent opened other doors as well. In Arizona he was introduced to one of his boyhood idols, General Nelson Miles. Miles, the distinguished Civil War veteran, was now a tough fighter of American Indians, in charge of finding Geronimo. The general and the young correspondent became friends. Miles wanted good publicity in *Harper's*. And Remington knew that Miles could give him valuable access to the army as it made news on the frontier.

An Artist in Training

The southwestern tour was the best possible on-the-job training for Remington. Dashing off dozens of black-and-white sketches, he was transforming himself into a full-time artist. On the trip he also began the habit of keeping an art journal. In it he jotted down descriptions of people and places and "color notes" that he would use for future paintings.

Under the cloudless sky, in the blistering sun, western colors were different from the softer tones of the East. In Arizona, the earth looked blue and red, with harsh shadows. In Mexico, Remington wrote, "It is impossible to get the white glare of the sun. . . ."[2]

Photography, too, helped him make accurate drawings. Everywhere he went, he took his bulky camera. (A lightweight Kodak model would not be available until 1889.) Although he was sometimes criticized for relying too much on photographs, Remington considered them just another research tool. Back in his studio the photos showed the smallest details, from the shape of a soldier's saddle to the feathers on a Cheyenne headdress. But snapshots could not come close to showing the kind of excitement that he wanted to convey. His drawings were often more dramatic than the real scene that had inspired them. Later in his career, as he used his camera less and less, Remington would sum it up this way: ". . . I can beat a Kodac [sic]—that is get more action and better action because Kodacs have no brains."[3]

Bringing the Indian Wars to Life in New York

The search for Geronimo finally ended, months after Remington returned to New York. In September 1886, the Apache leader and his weary followers surrendered to General Miles in Arizona. This chief, who had said, "Once I moved about like the wind,"[4] would spend the rest of his life a prisoner. Geronimo's people had held out longer than any other American Indian group, but now the Indian Wars of the Southwest had come to an end.

Back in New York, life for Remington was just beginning. He was breaking into the field of illustrating at an unheard-of speed. In addition to *Harper's*, other popular magazines were buying his drawings. Remington's friend Poultney Bigelow was now editing *Outing* magazine. When he saw Fred's southwestern work, he wrote that ". . . genius was in the rough drawings."[5] By the end of 1886, Remington's first year as a professional, twenty-five of his illustrations had been published.

What made him stand out from the crowd? Remington's pictures had high-spirited action quite unlike that found in other artists' work. His horses seemed to gallop faster, his fights appeared deadlier. He made no attempt to "prettify" his characters, either, but drew them the way he saw them.

He was working at almost superhuman speed now, as he would all his life. He could finish a picture in just a few hours. The pace would become so intense that Eva would one day comment, "Fred is working as hard as he would if he had 40 children hanging to his coat tails crying for bread."[6]

Home base would always be in the East because he needed to be near his publishers. But he could not stay away from the West for long: "If I sat around the house all the time I couldn't do it. . . . I must go somewhere and see something new."[7] At the start of his career, Remington set a pattern—alternating trips West with time at home, where he would create finished work from ideas he had gathered in his travels. The constant absences were hard on Eva, who would never have children to keep her busy. But Fred wrote constantly, calling her "My dear girl" or "Kid."

A Visit to the Crow and Blackfoot Indians

In 1887, Remington headed northwest through North Dakota and Wyoming. After visiting the Crow people, he made his way up to the Blackfoot reservation in Alberta, Canada. It was a good thing that he had his camera because the Blackfoot hated being sketched and were quick to tear up Remington's paper if they caught him drawing. This journey resulted in many pen-and-ink sketches and two magnificent oil paintings, *An Indian Trapper* and *Return of the Blackfoot War Party*.

An Indian Trapper is a splendid picture of a Blackfoot man involved in the fur trade. In *Return of the Blackfoot War Party*, a group of warriors comes home in the snow, bringing a scalp and two luckless captives with them. Remington's fine use of detail and atmosphere almost makes the viewer feel the sharp cold of the dark gray evening.

The Hallgarten Prize

In 1888, Remington exhibited *Return of the Blackfoot War Party* at New York's National

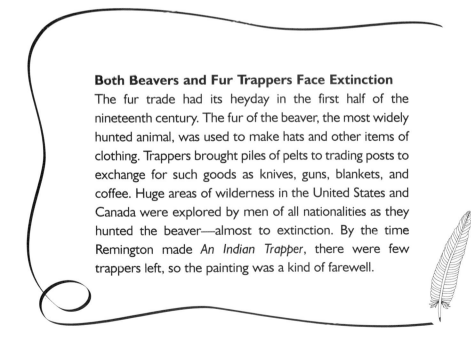

Both Beavers and Fur Trappers Face Extinction

The fur trade had its heyday in the first half of the nineteenth century. The fur of the beaver, the most widely hunted animal, was used to make hats and other items of clothing. Trappers brought piles of pelts to trading posts to exchange for such goods as knives, guns, blankets, and coffee. Huge areas of wilderness in the United States and Canada were explored by men of all nationalities as they hunted the beaver—almost to extinction. By the time Remington made *An Indian Trapper*, there were few trappers left, so the painting was a kind of farewell.

An Indian Trapper *was one of Frederic Remington's most famous depictions of a Blackfoot Indian.*

Academy of Design, an elite art society that included as members many of America's best painters, sculptors, and architects. The painting won the Hallgarten Prize, awarded every year to the most promising artist under thirty-five. One critic predicted that the young artist would become one of "our great American painters."[8]

This opinion suited Remington just fine. With each new accomplishment he became more ambitious. Not content to be known only as an illustrator, he wanted to make his mark in the high-status field of fine art, too. In the public's mind there was a great divide between the two worlds. An illustration is a picture made to accompany a story, and it often describes a very specific time and place, often a current event. But fine art has a more time-less and universal appeal.

But it was hard to make a living at fine art, whereas Remington's income from illustrating doubled between 1886 and 1887. In 1887, too, came an assignment that would give an enormous boost to his reputation.

Illustrating for Theodore Roosevelt

Wealthy young Theodore Roosevelt, also a lover of the West, had written a book about his years as a cattle rancher in North Dakota. Called *Ranch Life and the Hunting Trail*, it required many illustrations,

In a Stampede *was one of the many illustrations that Frederic Remington did for Theodore Roosevelt's* Ranch Life and the Hunting Trail.

and Roosevelt chose Remington to do them. One of them is called *An Episode in the Opening Up of a Cattle Country*. It shows a struggle for territory in the Old West. Cowboys are huddling behind their horses while American Indians circle on horseback, preparing to close in for the kill. This "last stand" theme is classic Remington, and he would paint many variations of it throughout his career.

"That's a pretty good break for an ex cowpuncher to come to New York with $30 and catch on in 'art,'" wrote Remington while he was working on the Roosevelt book.[9] Money from illustrating had enabled the Remingtons to move several times in New York City, each time to a nicer apartment.

Family Problems

Although Eva was happy with her husband's financial success, she was alone more and more. When he was not working, Remington loved to let off steam with his friends at The Players Club, a gathering place for prominent businessmen, artists, and writers. At the club he became close friends with the illustrator E. W. Kemble and the writer Julian Ralph, and there he would later meet the famous British writer Rudyard Kipling. Huge, festive dinners and plenty of whiskey brought Remington's weight to about two hundred and thirty pounds.

He was a man of strong likes and dislikes. Usually loyal to friends and family, he could be totally unforgiving when crossed. He showed this hard side to his mother when she remarried, in 1888. Clara Remington's new husband was Orris Levis, a hotelkeeper in Canton. Fred had strongly disapproved of the match, and when he could not prevent it, took his revenge. "I want Mrs. Levis to know that she is nothing to me," he announced.[10] And he never spoke to his mother again.

The Tenth Cavalry, San Carlos, and Indian Territory

Despite the break with his mother, Remington was itching to travel again in the summer of 1888. He persuaded *Century Magazine* to let him write and illustrate a series of articles on the American Indians of the Southwest. Most Americans knew next to nothing about this part of the country, so the articles would be real news—the nineteenth-century equivalent of our television documentaries.

Armed with his camera and sketchbook, Remington was glad to be wandering again. On this trip he would write articles that were full of colorful descriptions. He had turned to journalism just to create a market for his drawings, but he found that he was a natural storyteller.

In his article "A Scout with the Buffalo Soldiers," Remington describes a two-week ride through Arizona, his second visit with Lieutenant Clarke and the Tenth Cavalry. Overweight as he was, the scouting trip was grueling for Remington. On horseback the men scrambled up and down mountains so steep that one stumble could have plunged horse and rider to certain death. Plagued by mosquitoes and rattlesnakes, they plodded through the desert that was "hotter than any other place on the crust of the earth."[11] Remington went on to write, "On we marched over the rolling hills, dry, parched, desolate, covered with cactus and loose stones. It was Nature in one of her cruel moods, and the great silence over all the land displayed her mastery over man."[12]

Then he went to the San Carlos reservation. If the Apache saw it as an immense prison, Remington saw it mostly as an opportunity to observe and draw. In "On the Indian Reservations," he describes men galloping by, "with their long hair flying out behind,"[13] on their decorated ponies. One night he sat in the dark for hours, listening to the Apache's hypnotic drumming and singing: "It was more enjoyable in its way than any trained chorus I have ever heard," he wrote.[14]

The last stop was Indian Territory, a vast area in present-day Oklahoma that had been set aside for the many displaced tribes. There he met an old warrior named Chief Whirlwind. In "Artist Wandering Among the Cheyennes," Remington takes his most critical look yet at the problems of the conquered American Indians. He describes how white agents on the reservations often stole supplies meant for the Cheyenne. He also writes about the young American Indian men who, robbed of their hunting way of life, had nothing to do. Noting their exceptional bravery in battle, he recommends that they be allowed to join the U.S. Cavalry.

Attitudes on Race

Remington has often been called prejudiced. His private letters do reveal that he felt superior to African Americans, American Indians, Jews, and the masses of immigrants then coming to the United States. But he was a complex man, and in daily life was capable of judging people as individuals. His adventures with the Tenth Cavalry convinced him that the African-American soldiers were among the best in the army, loyal and brave. And in his art he almost always tried to draw without prejudice, but with an eye to truth.

His attitude toward American Indians is hard to pin down and is one of the mysteries of Remington's character. It seems to be a case of mixed feelings, all of them strong. He *always* sided with the army during the brutal Indian Wars. Yet he harshly criticized the injustices he saw on the reservations. And as

Remington grew older, his sensitivity increased. His stories and novels would show a keen understanding of many aspects of American Indian life. Most striking of all, the haunting paintings of his mature years would powerfully express the American Indians' sense of loss and their grieving for the old life.

Working All the Time

In 1888, scarcely a week went by without a Remington drawing in a popular magazine. It hardly seemed possible that he could top this success, but in 1889 he did.

He tackled his biggest assignment yet—making about five hundred pictures for a new edition of Henry Wadsworth Longfellow's 1855 poem "Hiawatha." He began the job near Canton, at Cranberry Lake in the Adirondacks. The lake was a favorite vacation spot of the Remingtons. Remington liked to paint in a boat on the peaceful water, with Eva for company. Or he would set up his easel on the shore. A family friend remembered how he tapped his foot and whistled nonstop as he worked: "Oh dear me, how we came to hate that whistle, it nearly drove us crazy."[15]

That summer too Remington learned that one of his cowboy-and-Indian paintings, *The Last Lull in the Fight*, had won the silver medal at the 1889 Paris International Exposition. It was rare for a painting of the American West to be taken that seriously, especially in Europe.

A Dash for the Timber

And in 1889, so early in his career, Remington painted one of his best-loved masterpieces—*A Dash for the Timber*. Commissioned by a wealthy man named E. C. Converse, the picture tells a tale of war on the frontier, and its unusually large size is well suited to its thundering action. Cowboys gallop for their lives toward a stand of trees, with Apache in furious pursuit. One cowboy, already shot, is being held up on his horse by his comrade. Whizzing bullets, gun smoke, pounding hooves, panic—Remington's paintbrush brought it all magically to life.

He worked hard to make his pictures seem real. In his New York studio, Remington did research to get the details just right. He often asked Powhatan Clarke to send him photographs and western items to serve as models. While working on *Dash*, he begged Clarke to send him some leather cowboy chaps: ". . . ship them to me by express C.O.D. I will be your slave."[16]

Horses were almost more important to Remington's art than people. Above all else he prided himself on his wonderful ability to paint them. He was probably the first American artist to make use of photographer Eadweard Muybridge's groundbreaking discovery. In a series of photographs taken in quick succession, Muybridge proved that all four of a horse's legs are off the ground at the same time at a certain point in the gallop. At this airborne instant front legs and back legs are tucked toward each other under the animal's belly.

Remington never gave Muybridge any credit, although *A Dash for the Timber* and many of his other pictures show careful study of the photographer's work. But Remington went further. He exaggerated the animals' movements for dramatic effect. In *Dash* the result is thrilling—a line of horses that seems about to charge straight at the viewer, unstoppable.

When the painting was exhibited at the National Academy of Design, *The New York Times* reported that it drew the largest crowds. Remington the illustrator had proven beyond a doubt that he could also paint.

"I am driven to death with work and hardly have time to breathe," he wrote in the eventful year of 1889.[17] But he would not have had it any other way. His ambition and his talent had paid off. He had progressed from his first "crude" sketches to the masterpiece *A Dash for the Timber* in just four years. Some Americans already recognized Remington as the leading artist of the West. He was twenty-eight years old.

5

THE END
OF THE
FRONTIER

Americans formed their ideas about the West largely from Remington's exciting images. Racing to keep up with the demand, he became a kind of "one-man industry" for pictures of the frontier. In the year 1890 alone, Harper's Weekly published 119 of his illustrations. Harper's Monthly, the company's literary magazine, printed thirty-six illustrations. Century Magazine, Harper's main rival, included eighteen illustrations. Remington's drawings also appeared in lesser-known periodicals and in books by several authors. Such high output made him rich. And with his new riches, he and Eva bought their first home, in New Rochelle, New York, and decorated it luxuriously.

Endion

"I wish you could see my house . . .," wrote Remington to Powhatan Clarke. "My head is getting large on account of it."[1] It was a big brick house, with a vine-covered porch and gingerbread carving on its pointed roof. Inside there was room for an art gallery, and outside was a garden, a henhouse, a tennis court, and stables for Remington's two horses. On three acres of trees and lawn, the hilltop location provided a view of Long Island Sound. Fred named his home Endion, which is an Algonquin word meaning "the place where I live."

For Remington the best thing about Endion was the enormous studio that he built several years after moving in. A skylight and windows let in floods of light. At one end of the studio's forty-foot length were double doors large enough to admit a horse. Floors and walls were jam-packed with the treasures that he had collected in his travels and used as models in his work. Among them were Mexican sombreros, silver, and pottery. There were cowboys' lariats, saddles, and hats and cavalry uniforms and weapons of all kinds. The American Indian collection was immense: beaded moccasins, snowshoes, war bonnets, peace pipes, tomahawks, and blood-stained arrows, to name a few. Over the fireplace hung the head of a moose; on the mantelpiece grinned a human skull. Surrounded by these mementos of the

Frederic Remington (left) stands with his bike while Eva sits on the porch of their home, Endion, in New Rochelle, New York.

West, Remington worked all day in a rocking chair in front of his easel. And as he worked, he whistled to the rhythm of his paintbrush.

But for Eva the best thing about Endion was the time that she and her "small boy" spent together. She was the calm center in the whirlwind of Remington's life. In New Rochelle they dug together in the garden. And when Remington was not feasting at The Players Club, they entertained friends at home. "We are just as happy as we can be . . .," wrote Eva.[2]

The Myth of Remington

Almost everything about Frederick Remington was on a large scale, including his publicity. He happily helped his publishers create wild myths about his past. *Harper's* promoted him as a soldier, as well as an artist, claiming that he had fought in the Indian Wars. The public also read that he had fired his six-shooter at outlaws and herded cattle with cowboys.

Actually, Remington hated the sight of blood.[3] He had ridden—not fought—with the cavalry, and he had absolutely never been a cowboy. His life's real mission was to observe. With his incredible eye for detail and drama, he was recording the West as it had never been done before. And about what he *saw*, he was totally honest. In spite of all the tall

tales, it was true when *Harper's* wrote, "He draws what he knows and he knows what he draws."[4]

Photoengraving and Oil Paintings

In the early 1890s a technical breakthrough occurred in the field of illustration that made Remington's drawings even more accessible to readers everywhere. It was called photoengraving, and it enabled one to create prints that were as much like the original drawing as possible. "It is one of those things that make an illustrator's life worth living," declared Remington.[5]

His oil paintings too were often reproduced by photoengraving to illustrate stories in magazines. (Until color photoengraving arrived later on in the decade, these prints were also in black and white.) But Remington was producing brilliant oils now, and he wanted them to be seen in higher circles, too, in the world of fine art. His paintings of the early 1890s were exhibited in New York and other cities and show a wide range of theme and mood.

Gentleman Rider on the Paseo de la Reforma, completed after a trip to Mexico, is richly colored and lighthearted. An elegantly dressed Mexican surveys the passing carriages as he prances down the boulevard on his spirited white horse. Even the horse's shadow seems to dance.

The Evolution of Engraving

Before photoengraving was invented, illustrations were reproduced in magazines by means of wood engravings. Professional wood engravers copied the lines of a drawing onto a block of wood, which was then rubbed with ink and placed in a printing press. There the image was transferred, or printed, onto paper. It was actually the wood engraver's copy of the drawing that was published. Photoengraving eliminated the wood engraver's job. In this new method a photograph was taken of the drawing to be reproduced. The negative that resulted was pressed against a copper plate that had been treated with light-sensitive chemicals. A quick exposure to light transferred the image on the negative onto the copper plate. After the printer dipped the plate into an acid bath, the image—the artist's drawing— stood out against the copper background. Then the plate was ready to be inked and printed, just like an engraved woodblock.

What a different mood is struck in the 1890 picture *The Scout: Friends or Enemies?* A scout on horseback looks out over the snow-covered prairie at a distant village, wondering if it is safe for him to approach. This is what the Old West was like, Remington seems to say—dangerous and cold. The stars sparkling over the empty land increase the feelings of loneliness and awe.

About the same time, Remington painted one of his most famous military pictures, *A Cavalryman's Breakfast on the Plains*. It shows a moment in the daily life of the army that fought the American Indians. Although Remington was friendly with many of the army's elite, such as General Nelson Miles, he also deeply respected the common soldiers and loved to travel with them, sharing their hardships and humor. In this carefully composed scene, the men are clustered in groups, getting ready for a long day's ride.

Back to Montana

General Miles invited Remington to Montana in the fall of 1890, so the artist was soon back with his beloved cavalry. On his arrival he made an unforgettable impression on a young lieutenant named Alvin Sydenham. Sydenham wrote:

> We first became aware of his existence in camp by the unusual spectacle of a fat citizen dismounting from a tall troop horse at the head of a column of cavalry. . . . As he ambled toward camp, his gait was an easy graceful waddle. . . . Fair complexion, blue eyes, light hair, smooth face . . . a big, good-natured overgrown boy—a fellow you could not fail to like the first time you saw him. . . . [6]

Remington had a blonde mustache. When he was not wearing his English safari helmet, he sported a floppy felt hat, and his canvas coat stretched over his round body like a "brown cotton umbrella."[7] Among the tough, lean men of the cavalry, he enjoyed playing the role of a "character."

The Ghost Dance

While Remington was in Montana, trouble between the U.S. government and the Sioux was coming to a head. Recently the government had divided up the Great Sioux Reservation, taking away millions of acres of land that had been granted in the Treaty of 1868. At the same time Congress had cut the tribe's food allotments, hoping to encourage them to take up farming. But crops withered and died in the dry Dakota soil. And there were no more buffalo to hunt. Confined and hungry, the Sioux were in despair. No new life had come to take the place of the one that was gone. To many it seemed that only a miracle could help.

Wovoka, a Paiute Indian from Nevada, offered one in the form of a new religion. He taught his followers the Ghost Dance and promised that if they kept on dancing, something wonderful would occur. In the green springtime of 1891, he said, the soil would rise up and cover every last trace of white civilization. The American Indians' ancestors would return to Earth to enjoy eternal life with their tribes. The vanished buffalo, the elk, and antelope too would once again cover the prairie. All would be as it had been before, only better. In the meantime, if the dancers wore special "ghost shirts," the bullets of the soldiers could not harm them.

Many American Indians called Wovoka the Messiah. The Ghost Dance religion swept through the reservations, and many people dropped everything to dance. Among the Sioux, some young men wanted to fight the army. Rumors flew. Remington sent *Harper's Weekly* a sketch of the Ghost Dance being performed, and soon the magazine was predicting "the bloodiest Indian War ever fought."[8]

The Death of Sitting Bull

General Miles hoped to stop the movement without bloodshed, but he feared that the Sioux would flee the reservations in "one final effort in the death struggle of their race."[9] Because Sitting Bull was involved, Miles ordered his arrest. But during the arrest, on December 15, 1890, the great chief was killed.

In the anger and panic that followed, some American Indians left the reservations, while others tried to avoid trouble by moving closer to the agencies, or reservation headquarters. A detachment of the Seventh Cavalry, Custer's old regiment, caught up with a peaceful band of Sioux and made them camp overnight at Wounded Knee Creek, in South Dakota. On the freezing morning of December 29,

1890, as soldiers tried to disarm the Sioux, shooting broke out. (Some historians say that a Sioux gun fired first, accidentally.)[10] The cavalry let loose its powerful cannons. When the firing was over, at least one hundred and fifty Sioux men, women, and children were dead. The ghost shirts had failed to protect them.

In his old age Black Elk, a holy man and relative of Crazy Horse, remembered the scene.

> I can still see the butchered women and children lying heaped and scattered all along the crooked gulch as plain as when I saw them with eyes still young. And I can see that something else died there in the bloody mud, and was buried in the blizzard. A people's dream died there. It was a beautiful dream. . . ."[11]

The incident at Wounded Knee ended the Ghost Dance religion, and it ended the American Indians' last hope that they might regain their freedom. The United States had complete control of the West now; it was the end of the frontier.

Remington Reports on Wounded Knee

Immediately after Sitting Bull's death, *Harper's* had instructed Remington to report on the trouble. But when the massacre occurred, he was miles away, camping with his friend Lieutenant Casey and his Cheyenne scouts. Remington arrived at the camp of the Seventh Cavalry on New Year's Day, 1891. After hearing the soldiers' firsthand accounts of Wounded

Knee, he drew a picture and wrote an article entitled "The Sioux Outbreak in South Dakota."

The article takes the army's point of view and shows Remington at the height of his cavalry worship. At another time he had talked of the government's "oppressing a conquered people."[12] Now he praised an officer's coolness in action:

> This professional interest in the military process of killing men sometimes rasps a citizen's nerves. To the captain everything else was a side note of little consequence so long as his guns had been worked to his entire satisfaction. That was the point.[13]

Curiously, two years after Wounded Knee, Remington painted a picture that was powerfully sympathetic to the American Indians. *Conjuring Back the Buffalo* is an image of grief. A young warrior raises a buffalo skull to the sky and calls to the Great Spirit to bring back the herds. But he knows they will not return.

Troubles in Europe

Now that the Indian Wars were over, Remington needed new sources of inspiration. He accepted an invitation from his old Yale friend, writer, and editor Poultney Bigelow, to go to Europe. Bigelow (known as "Big"), a canoe enthusiast like Remington, planned a canoe trip on Russia's Volga River. Two fancy canoes, complete with sails and a sleeping compartment, were specially made for the voyage.

Remington also hoped to sketch the armies of the Russian leader Czar Alexander III, and the German emperor Wilhelm II. Maybe he would even see a battle. But he confessed to Powhatan Clarke that he did not think he would like Europe: "I was born in the woods and the higher they get the buildings the worse I like them."[14]

In May 1892, Remington and Bigelow crossed the Atlantic Ocean on a steamship. Although the trip began with caviar and champagne toasts, it soon turned into a disaster. In St. Petersburg the two Americans were suspected of being spies. They were followed everywhere by the czar's secret police, and their mail was opened. They could not even get permission for their canoe trip. Remington was becoming more frightened by the minute and impatient to leave the country. He soon got his wish, because he and Bigelow were expelled from Russia.

The next stop was Germany, where Remington sketched the emperor's soldiers on their magnificent horses. In Paris, where he went alone, he felt lost. The miserable trip ended in London, where at least Buffalo Bill's Wild West Show was in town. Although it amused the famous western artist, the greatest relief for him was to sail home.

In Europe, Remington had gathered a huge amount of material to illustrate articles. Still the experience only confirmed in his mind what he had suspected all along—he hated Europe. ". . . America is the only place on the Earth which is worth the efforts of men in the Grace of God," he wrote.[15] Even five years after the trip, he would cheerfully write the following to Bigelow: "No, honey—I shall not try Europe again. . . . I hate parks, collars, cuffs, foreign languages, cut and dried stuff. No, Bigelow . . . I am going to do America—it's new—it's to my taste."[16]

Vacationing in New York

After his return from Europe, the Remingtons hurried to the North Country, where they liked to spend part of every summer. In the land of his childhood, Fred still felt at home. He laughed with old friends in Canton and Ogdensburg and gave them presents of his artwork. And the natives appreciated that even though Remington was famous, he was not at all "stuck up." At Cranberry Lake, when he was not painting or writing, he played hard. As much as possible he tramped around outdoors with his friends Bill and Has Rasbeck, both Adirondack guides. The three men hunted for bear, took canoe trips, and fished for speckled trout. The West was where Remington found adventure and inspiration, but the clear waters of the North Country brought him peace.

"Remington never stays put for long in any one place, but there's an awful lot of him while he's around," commented Has Rasbeck fondly.[17] At his wife's urging, Remington kept on battling his obsessive eating and drinking. But he could never control himself for long. Too often he gave in to his craving for whiskey and pork—pigs' knuckles, spareribs, roast pork dripping with gravy. A waitress at Cranberry Lake's hotel remembered that he had needed two chairs placed close together to support his weight. "His big bottom would fill them both, and how that man would eat. My, my, my, how that man would eat!"[18]

Wealth and an Artist's Style

Remington's cravings were often out of control, but his career never was. In January 1893, he held an auction in New York, offering about one hundred works for sale. Watercolors, drawings, and oil paintings sold for slightly less than he had hoped, but the sheer volume of pictures sold brought the total to more than seven thousand dollars. "A decided art triumph," he called it.[19]

His output in the early 1890s had been enormous, and by now he was one of the wealthiest artists in America. But he had made his reputation as an illustrator, a "black-and-white man." Real fame as an oil painter was still maddeningly out of reach.

Frederic Remington sits at an easel in his studio, which is filled with various items from the American West.

In fine art the two most respected movements of the day were Tonalism and Impressionism. Painters of the Tonalist school tried to achieve a beautiful, spiritual effect by making landscapes in which most of the colors were subtle variations of one tone. By 1886, Impressionism had only recently been introduced to Americans. Impressionist painters favored soft, blurry outlines and choppy brushstrokes. For artists like Monet and Renoir, the dazzling effects of light and color were just as important as the subjects they were painting.

Not so for Remington. He was out of step with both styles in the 1890s. He wanted his paintings to tell a story—the story of men fighting each other for land or fighting to survive the cruel weather of the West. The struggles usually occurred on horseback, and only the strong survived. Some critics complained that his pictures were too full of the "screams of dying horses" and the "yells of battle."[20] But he would not change to please them. "I was born wanting to do certain phases of life and I am going to die doing them."[21]

6

COWBOYS

Remington began the year 1893 in the wilds of northern Mexico, far from crowded cities and art critics. He had already been there several times, and before he left, he wrote to Poultney Bigelow, ". . . tomorrow I start for 'my people' . . . I go to the simple men—men with the bark on—the big mountains—the great deserts and the scrawny ponies—I'm happy."[1] His traveling companion was Will Harper, who with his brother Henry owned Harper & Brothers publishing company. This was also one of the few trips on which Eva accompanied her husband, if only part of the way. She left the men when the train arrived in Detroit and set out to visit friends and relatives in mid-western cities.

Harper and Remington pushed south by train, stage-coach, and horseback. After a dusty, bone-shaking journey over hills and dry riverbeds, they reached their destination—San José de Bavicora, a sprawling ranch in Mexico, near the Sierra Madre Mountains.

The Vaqueros of Mexico

The one hundred thousand-acre spread belonged to a Texan named Jack Follansbee, who ruled his estate, Remington observed, like some lord or king. Only a few years ago, this had been Geronimo's territory. Now the danger to Follansbee and his two hundred vaqueros (Spanish for "cowboys") came mostly from cattle rustlers and other outlaws. The ranch was miles from any other settlements; it took two weeks just to ride around its borders. Listening to wolves howling in the black night, Remington felt as if he had traveled back in time to the early frontier days of the Old West.

His weeks at Bavicora resulted in four illustrated articles, commissioned by *Harper's*. In "An Outpost of Civilization," printed in *Harper's Monthly*, Remington humorously describes the perils of his stagecoach ride to the ranch:

> . . . the Guerrero stage has never failed to tip over, and the company makes you sign away your natural rights, and almost your immortal soul, before it will allow you to embark. . . . We had a coach which seemed to choose the steepest hill on the route, where it then

struck a stone, which heaved the coach, pulled out the king-pin, and what I remember of the occurrence is full of sprains and aches and general gloom. . . .[2]

In the article Remington also writes of a slow-paced world of burros, dogs, and people, lazing in the shimmering heat. The quiet was sometimes shattered, though, as he shows in his pen-and-ink drawing *Mexican Vaqueros Breaking a Bronc*. The black-eyed vaqueros were the most skilled cowboys he had ever seen. They made their own saddles and lariats. And no one could rope a steer as expertly or tame a horse better than they. In their sombreros and spurs, they were the stars of the ranch.

Remington drew all day long, storing up a wealth of ideas for paintings. Everywhere he looked, he saw "The marvellous color of the country. . . ."[3] Men draped boldly striped serapes (woolen blankets) over their shoulders, and women wore colorful dresses with bright blue shawls. The old adobe buildings and the dry plains were yellow, and in the distance loomed the violet-colored Sierra Madre Mountains. He sketched an exciting rodeo one day. One night there was a dance. Remington watched as vaqueros and their girlfriends whirled to the music of a lively string band. San José de Bavicora was a place he would never forget.

Remembering Powhatan Clarke

Back at Endion in the summertime, Remington heard tragic news. Lieutenant Powhatan Clarke had drowned on July 21, in the Little Bighorn River. He had been teaching a group of soldiers stationed at Fort Custer, Montana, to swim. "I cannot and never will be used to the idea that my friend Clarke is dead," wrote Remington.[4]

He had always thought of Clarke as the ideal man, a soldier of great courage, and he had painted a handsome portrait of him. The two men had actually seen each other only three times, but they had been great friends. They had had a rich correspondence, with Remington sprinkling his many letters with cartoon-like drawings. They had discussed everything from the proper design of army uniforms to Fred's latest painting. Clarke had also provided the artist with valuable information about life in the West. He had sent to New Rochelle photographs, written descriptions, and many items used by American Indians, cowboys, and soldiers. "MAKE NOTES—MAKE NOTES—MAKE NOTES!" Remington had urged Clarke when he needed help with his research.[5]

Artist Meets Writer

Nothing could fill the gap left by Clarke. But later that summer, at Yellowstone National Park, Remington met Owen Wister, another man who would have a profound effect on his life. Although trained as a lawyer, Wister had turned to writing as his real love. He had chosen for his subject the Wild West, and he aimed to do for that region with words what Remington was doing with pictures. As he began writing western stories, Wister hoped for "the joy of being illustrated by Frederic Remington."[6] He got his wish. By the time the men met, *Harper's* had already paid Remington to illustrate one of Wister's cowboy tales. The artist and the writer quickly became friends.

The two were as different as night and day. Owen Wister was a wealthy, Harvard-educated Philadelphian. He was at home in fine mansions and glittering opera houses. Remington, on the other hand, had dropped out of Yale after one and a half years and was only truly happy outdoors. Although only one year older than Remington, Wister had first gone West to improve his ill health. The frail writer generally looked on the gloomy side of things; he was in awe of Remington's bouncing high spirits. At their first meeting he noted that "Remington weighs about 240 pounds and is a huge, rollicking animal."[7]

Yet they both loved the West and mourned the old frontier days. They agreed that the United States was becoming too industrialized, and, as Wister put it, turning into "merely a strip of land on which a crowd is struggling for riches."[8] They rode

Owen Wister (pictured) quickly became Frederic Remington's friend. This photo was taken at Mammoth Hot Springs in Yellowstone National Park on August 29, 1891.

part of the way back East on the same train, talking about the projects they hoped to do together.

The Gilded Age

Remington stopped alone in Chicago to see the World's Columbian Exposition, or Chicago World's Fair. He toured the fair's Art Building, where, although almost every well-known American artist was represented, there were only fifteen Remington illustrations. And he had not submitted any oils. But pictures with western themes attracted little attention, anyway. People crowded around the Impressionist paintings instead. In keeping with the mood of the fair, they were more interested in modern art movements than in images of the American past.

Was Remington at the fair when the historian Frederick Jackson Turner announced that the American frontier was closed? If not, he knew it

Chicago World's Fair

The Chicago World's Fair was the most spectacular event of 1893, with about 28 million people coming to walk among the fairground's splashing fountains and ornate white buildings. An amusement area called the Midway contained exotic wonders from all over the world—the most popular of which was an Egyptian belly-dancing show. But the fair was also an exciting celebration of everything American. The country's rapid technological progress was on proud display everywhere. There was a large exhibit devoted to the uses of electricity, from Edison's light bulb to the first dishwasher. And visitors rode on the world's first Ferris wheel, two hundred feet high.

already, for he had watched the soldiers return from the frozen burial ground at Wounded Knee. By 1893, the United States had completed its Manifest Destiny. There were forty-four states now, and what land remained was organized into territories. The days of wagon trains in the wilderness were over.

It was the era that Mark Twain called the Gilded Age. Men like J. P. Morgan and John D. Rockefeller were making fabulous fortunes. Industry, fueled by immigrant labor, was expanding to change forever the way Americans lived. To Remington's disgust the new national passion was the future and all the wealth that business and urban life could bring.

He avoided cities like a disease. It would kill him, he said, if he had to live among crowds for long.[9] No sooner had he come home from the Chicago fair than he was off to the wild places again. Within one year he would hunt deer in Virginia with Julian Ralph and grizzly bears in New Mexico with Nelson Miles. He even broke his vow never to cross the ocean again and went sketching in North Africa with Poultney Bigelow. And that was not all. Many who knew him wondered how he found time for his art. Actually, he never really stopped working. Each adventure provided him with fresh ideas for pictures.

A Creative Collaboration

Illustration was still the main source of Remington's high income, but he preferred not having to write his own articles. Late in 1893 he plunged enthusiastically into a collaboration with Owen Wister. It would last until 1902—a source of inspiration, friendship, and sometimes frustration for both men.

They were a good team. But Wister liked to take his time, while Remington did everything as fast as lightning. Amused by his new friend's cautious personality, Remington gave him nicknames like Nerve-Cell and War Eagle. He was always pushing Wister to crank out more words, faster: ". . . please get a move on—I am starving. . . ."[10] The pushing helped. In 1894, both *Harper's Weekly* and *Harper's Monthly* were filled with Wister's cowboy stories, vividly illustrated by Remington.

In the beginning, Wister needed some help getting the details right. What does a man say when he is wounded in a gunfight? asked the civilized Philadelphian. Most of them say, "My God—I'm shot," Remington replied.[11] In another letter he advised Wister jokingly, "Put every person on horseback and let the blood be half a foot deep. Be very profane and have plenty of shooting. No episode must occur in the dark."[12]

"The Evolution of a Cowpuncher"

Cowboys, cowpunchers, trail drivers, wranglers—whatever name was used, Americans were fascinated by the men who herded cattle for a living. Remington had increasingly turned his attention to them as the Indian Wars ended, leaving the cavalry with little to do out West. By the 1890s the golden days of the cowboy were over too, but the Wister-Remington stories were selling well. "Cowboys are cash," the ever-practical artist would soon write.[13]

Aside from practical matters Remington loved the cowboy and his horse almost as much as he loved the soldier. Since his earliest professional days—and before—he had sketched and painted them. Some of his best works would be wranglers in paint and bronze. And other fine cowboy artists, such as Charles Russell, would always be seen as following in Remington's footsteps. If Wister would write a short history of the cowpuncher, Remington thought, he could illustrate it with dramatic pictures: "Write me something where I can turn myself loose. Tell the story of the cowpuncher, his rise and decline."[14] The two men met at Endion to discuss the project, and Wister said yes.

Remington immediately showered him with facts about cowboys learned from research and first-hand observation. The first ones, he explained, were the hard-riding vaqueros from Mexico. In time, some of the vaqueros moved north to find work on the rich grasslands of California and Texas.

In those early years, longhorn cattle grazed wild on the plains. Ranch owners hired cowboys to round them up and brand them. But the West had always been buffalo country. As cattle threatened their own food source, American Indians clashed with cowboys. In *A Dash for the Timber* and the 1901 picture *Fight for the Waterhole*, Remington shows that the life of a cowpuncher in the Old West could be violent—and short.

After the Civil War the cattle boom spread as far north as Wyoming and Montana. By the 1880s, the buffalo were gone; the beef herds were king of the range. On trails as long as one thousand miles, cowboys drove the bellowing steers to the railyards of Kansas for shipment to the slaughterhouses.

All kinds of young men applied for the job of wrangler, including immigrants from Europe, African Americans, and American Indians. They were a hardy bunch, with an appetite for freedom and for life on horseback. In picture after picture Remington shows them taming broncos, roping steers, riding the rodeo, or galloping in for a night on the town. A good cowboy could calm his cattle at night by singing to them. He also had to face real danger, one of the most dreaded events being a stampede. In Remington's great 1909 painting

In The Stampede, *a cowboy frantically tries to control a frightened herd of cattle.*

The Stampede, a crack of thunder has made the herd panic. The artist shows a cowpuncher trying desperately to control the rushing animals while risking being crushed to a pulp under the pounding hooves.

In spite of Remington's help, it took Owen Wister nearly a year—and a lot of nagging from his friend—to finish his cowboy history. "The Evolution of the Cowpuncher" was published in *Harper's Monthly* in September 1895, with five illustrations by Remington. It was the finest achievement of the two-man team, and it made Wister famous.

The Death of the Cowboy?

The era of the open range was short. An oversupply of cattle caused ranchers to compete for pasture land, so barbed-wire fences sprouted up, sectioning off large parcels of prairie. Then, in the winters of 1885 and 1886, enormous blizzards swept over the West, turning it into a white and frozen silence. Almost 90 percent of the herds died, and when the industry was rebuilt, it would be far more controlled. The romantic days when the cowboys rode the unfenced land were over. According to Remington, the "real" cowboy had mostly disappeared by the late 1880s, along with the free American Indian and the fur-trapping mountain man.

Although Remington complained that his friend had not given enough credit to the Mexican vaqueros for being the first cowboys, Wister had used much of Remington's information and even some of Remington's own words. The result was a classic essay, the first of its kind. The brave and honest cowboy it described took a permanent hold on the American imagination. Part romance, part fact, he still gallops through books, movies, advertisements, and television shows today.

Among the five pictures that Remington made for "The Evolution of the Cowpuncher" is one of his most beautiful paintings, *The Fall of the Cowboy*. On a cold winter afternoon, under a threatening sky, two tired cowboys come home to the ranch. But it is a ranch enclosed by miles of barbed-wire fence, and they have to open a gate to get in. Quiet in color and mood, the picture is unusual for Remington in the mid-1890s, for there is no violent action. Instead it is like a sad cowboy ballad. It echoes the artist's feeling that the cowboys' best days are gone and seems to say, as Remington did, "Don't mistake

Frederic Remington's The Fall of the Cowboy *was one of the five paintings that was used to illustrate Owen Wister's article "The Evolution of the Cowpuncher."*

the nice young men who amble around wire fences for the 'wild riders of the Plains.'"[15]

Three Famous Friends

The year that Wister's essay was published, Theodore Roosevelt wrote to Remington, "It seems to me that you in your line, and Wister in his, are doing the best work in America today."[16]

All three men were friends. Roosevelt and Wister had met at Harvard. And back in 1887, Roosevelt had given Remington an important career boost, the job of illustrating his book *Ranch Life and the Hunting Trail*. Now the three easterners were the nation's most popular authorities on the West—Roosevelt for his nonfiction, Wister for his stories, and Remington for his art. Although Roosevelt was busy working his way up the political ladder all the way to the presidency, he remained a westerner at heart. In 1897, while he was Assistant Secretary of the Navy, he wrote to Remington, "I wish I were with you out among the sage brush."[17] The famous politician would always be one of Remington's biggest fans.

"I AM TO ENDURE IN BRONZE"

While Wister was writing about cowboys, Remington made a discovery that would change his life—sculpture. This new passion would result in what many say is the most important work of his career. For a while, it would put everything else in the shade.

Entry Into the World of Sculpture

It all started when Remington's neighbor, the playwright Augustus Thomas, visited the studio at Endion. Thomas watched as Remington drew and redrew the figures in a gunfight scene, experimenting with their placement in the picture. He noticed that the artist had no trouble visualizing his composition "in the round," a skill that all good sculptors possessed. "Fred, you're not a draftsman; you're a sculptor," he remarked to Remington. "You saw all round that fellow, and could have put him anywhere you wanted him."[1]

The thought of becoming a sculptor, casting clay models into bronze, intrigued Remington. He was tired of illustrating. After ten years he had reached the top of the field, and it all seemed too commercial to him now. But painting alone could not support his expensive lifestyle. It was time for something new.

Augustus Thomas's friend, the sculptor Frederick Ruckstull, also encouraged Remington and cautioned him not to worry too much about the mysteries of technique: "You see, in your mind, so very clearly anything that you want to draw. You will be able to draw just as clearly in wax [clay] as you do on paper."[2] Ruckstull even ordered all the equipment that Remington would need—clay, sculpting tools, and wire for the armature, or skeleton, of a piece.

The Bronco Buster

Soon Remington's hands were deep in the waxy modeling clay. He called it "mud." Wrestling with the clay, pounding and coaxing it into shape, suited his active personality. To Eva he declared happily, "Kid, I think I have found something."[3]

He had. A cowboy on a bucking bronco would be the first of the twenty-two subjects that he would sculpt. It was fitting that a rearing horse was his inspiration. No one had ever sculpted a "bronc" before, but Remington felt in his bones that his would be great. In January 1895 he wrote Owen Wister a letter decorated with a little sketch of his horse and rider. Even though he had only just begun, he teased Wister with some Remington-sized boasts and rejoiced in the permanence of bronze: "My oils will all get old and watery . . . my watercolors will fade—but I am to endure in bronze . . . I am doing a cowboy on a bucking bronco and I am going to rattle down through all the ages."[4]

Actually it was the hardest thing he had ever done. Most horse-themed statues in Remington's day were of dignified generals or statesmen, sitting motionless on horses whose hooves were solidly on the ground. But Remington wanted to show action. His bronco, rearing up almost vertically on its hind legs, was very difficult for a sculptor to balance. The headstrong beginner refused to change its position or use the traditional supporting post to keep the horse in place. Because he knew little about conventional sculpture, he had conceived of something totally new. Five frustrating months passed, but he made little progress.

Help came once again from Frederick Ruckstull. The sculptor had come to New Rochelle to work on his own statue in Augustus Thomas's backyard. He advised Remington to double the size of his armature, from twelve inches to twenty-four inches, and to shift slightly the weight of the rearing bronco. To Remington's joy the balance problem was solved. Nothing could stop him now. His hands flew, magically turning the mound of "mud" into a detailed horse and rider. By August 1895, *The Bronco Buster* (or *Broncho Buster*, as Remington spelled it) was finished.

But this was just the first step. Next Remington made a plaster cast of the clay piece and brought it to the Henry-Bonnard Bronze Company, a well-known foundry, or ironworks, in New York City. There, after much painstaking work, the two-foot high statuette was brought at last to its final form—a beautifully polished piece of bronze.

Remington's little horse rears up on its hind legs, with mouth open and forelegs pawing the air, desperate to throw off its rider. But the cowboy is just as determined to hang on. He grips with his knees, grabbing the horse's mane with one hand and waving his "quirt" (whip) in the other. From hat to hoof the statuette is amazingly true to life. Viewers often wonder who is meant to win the contest: horse or rider?

"Is there anything that man can't do!" exclaimed another artist when he heard that Remington had

The Bronzing Process

Creating a bronze is a process that involves several stages. First, a plaster cast is made by spreading glue over the entire clay model. When the glue hardens, it forms a mold, the inside of which holds the shape of the sculpture. The mold is then removed from the clay and reassembled. Liquid plaster is poured inside.

When the plaster dries it is time for sand casting. Workers cut the plaster into neat sections and press each piece into firm, claylike sand. The sand now holds perfect impressions of the artist's work. After the sand molds are baked hard in a type of oven called a kiln, hot, molten bronze is poured into them. When the bronze pieces cool, they are fitted together with special pins, to form once again the original shape of the sculpture.

The workers then file away rough spots and apply the chemicals that give the sculpture its color, or patina.

begun to sculpt.[5] *The Bronco Buster,* copyrighted just before Remington's thirty-fourth birthday, stunned the art world. It was the first bronze of a cowboy on a horse. It was also the first piece of sculpture to show such energy and action. Not only did it portray a piece of western history, but it made history itself. The self-taught sculptor had translated his love of cowboy and horse into an American original.

Most reviewers were full of praise, excited by Remington's new and unexpected talent. A few

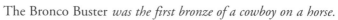

The Bronco Buster *was the first bronze of a cowboy on a horse.*

critics complained that the little statue was too realistic, not imaginative enough. They called it "illustration in-the-round." However, the public was delighted with *The Bronco Buster* because it captured the spirit of the West. It became Remington's most popular bronze and is probably still the most famous sculpture in America today.

While a painting is a one-of-a-kind piece of work, many casts of an original sculpture can be made. The Henry-Bonnard Bronze Company produced more than sixty *Buster* bronzes and sold them profitably, for $250 apiece, at Tiffany's in New York.

Thrilled with his success, Remington planned to do more sculpture, to show the West in work that "burglar won't have moth eat, or time blacken."[6] To Wister he wrote that "mud" was all he could think of now: ". . . all other forms of art are trivialities."[7]

More Bronzes

Remington completed more bronzes—*The Wounded Bunkie* in 1896 and *The Wicked Pony* and *The Scalp* two years later. He was most excited about *The Wounded Bunkie* because its theme was his favorite, the cavalry facing danger during the Indian Wars. The sculpture depicts two "bunkies," or comrades, galloping away from an unseen enemy. As in the painting *A Dash for the Timber*, one of them has been shot and is being supported by his friend. So close is the bond between the two soldiers that they will either escape or be killed, together. *The Wounded Bunkie* is so lifelike that veins can be seen bulging on the horses' necks. It is even more of a balancing miracle than *The Bronco Buster* because only two out of eight horses' legs touch the "ground."

Pony Tracks

The year of *The Bronco Buster*, 1895, was one of the peak years of Remington's life. He was busier than ever, as one project followed another, like horses in a headlong race. His illustrating work with Wister had slowed to a trickle because he was also painting, sculpting, and writing. In this year *Pony Tracks*, the first of eight Remington books, was published.

Dedicated to "the fellows who rode the ponies that made the tracks," *Pony Tracks* is a collection of fifteen previously printed articles about the West. The anthology includes accounts of the author's Mexican adventures and his grizzly-bear hunt with General Miles, but the main theme is soldiering. These literary sketches are more than straight journalistic reports. Full of Remington's opinions and witty observations, they are as entertaining as a good short story.

One reviewer thought that the book gave "a better idea of army life on the western border than all the official records that were ever written."[8]

Certainly Remington knew the cavalrymen as well as it was possible for a civilian to know them. He had lived with the soldiers, eating his breakfast at their campfires and riding with them up mountains and through blistering deserts. *Pony Tracks* sold well and was followed by two more anthologies, *Crooked Trails* in 1898 and *Men with the Bark On* in 1900.

An Artist's Frustration

Also in 1895, Remington organized an auction of his drawings and paintings at New York's American Art Association. It was his third such auction, and he hoped to sell everything. Theodore Roosevelt attended the exhibit and wrote to Remington, "I never so wished to be a millionaire . . . as when you have pictures to sell."[9] But profits would not be as high as Remington had expected. Out of 114 pictures for sale, most were drawings or black-and-white oil paintings done for illustration. Only ten pictures were oils in color, and this scarcity rekindled the artist's frustrations with his painting career.

He was angry at the National Academy of Design. From time to time, since 1887, he had shown paintings at the prestigious institution, and in 1891 its directors had made him an associate member. But they would never award him their highest honor, the title of "Academician." It was a strange gap in the career of an artist so talented. Had he not exhibited there often enough? Certainly the art establishment objected to his storytelling approach to painting. After 1899, Remington would refuse to exhibit at the Academy again. Fame as an oil painter, he realized, would have to come without the official blessing.

But he was not satisfied with his ability to paint color and partly agreed with critics who called some of his tones brittle, harsh, or flat. Too much black-and-white work and all his hours with clay had held back his progress with oil, Remington thought: "I can't tell a red blanket from a grey overcoat."[10] His unhappiness grew as he began to admire the American Impressionists, whose beautiful hues glowed softly on their canvases. In 1896 he planned an all-out attack on the problem. He would travel West and force himself to see colors again "with the wide open eyes of a child."[11]

Through the Smoke Sprang the Daring Soldier

In Montana, Remington stayed with his friend Lieutenant Carter Johnson, whom he had met in Arizona on the 1888 excursion with the buffalo soldiers. As he had in 1888, Johnson talked about his experiences during the Indian Wars. When Remington returned home, he put the lieutenant's memories on canvas in the 1897 painting *Through the Smoke Sprang the Daring Soldier*. It depicts one of the last fights between the northern Cheyenne and the army.

In a dramatic moment near the end of the stand-off, Lieutenant Johnson himself, with a gun in each hand, charges alone toward the Cheyenne and fires the winning shots.

The picture tells the tale from the soldiers' point of view; the Cheyenne are not seen. But in the related *Harper's Monthly* article, "A Sergeant of the Orphan Troop," Remington describes Lieutenant

Dull Knife, Little Wolf, and the Cheyenne

In 1878, a group of about three hundred Cheyenne men, women, and children, led by Dull Knife and Little Wolf, fled from the reservation in Indian Territory, where their people were dying of disease and starvation. They headed north for their old home in the Montana Territory, with the army in hot pursuit. ("Better it was, we thought, to die fighting than to perish of sickness," said Dull Knife.)[12] The Cheyenne got as far as Nebraska, when in the bitter January cold, they were cornered by the cavalry. They chose to fight to the death rather than return to Indian Territory.

Johnson's impression of the scene after the army's victory: "Buffalo robes lay all about, blood spotted everywhere. The dead bodies of thirty-two Cheyennes lay, writhed and twisted, on the packed snow, and among them many women and children, cut and furrowed with lead."[13]

Through the Smoke was Remington's first painting to be reproduced by the latest technique—color photoengraving. This was a piece of good luck for the artist. The blue and yellow soldiers' uniforms contrast powerfully with the pale sky and the trampled snow on the ground. The air is hazy with mingled puffs of snow and smoke. Remington was indeed making progress in his struggles with color.

But he was taking most of his subjects from the past. The war with the Cheyenne had occurred almost twenty years earlier, and Remington wanted to witness—and paint—a modern battle. As he wrote to Poultney Bigelow, "I live in the hope of a war."[14] There was trouble brewing between the United States and Spain over the Spanish colony of Cuba, and Remington wanted to be in the thick of the action.

8

WAR IN CUBA

S ince the days of Christopher Columbus, the island of Cuba had been ruled by Spain. But during Remington's lifetime Cubans were fighting for independence, with uprisings in the 1860s and 1870s. When José Martí led a fierce revolt in 1895, the Spanish sent General Valeriano Weyler to stop it. He quickly earned a reputation as "the Butcher" as he forced thousands of Cubans into concentration camps. Herded together in miserable conditions, they died of diseases such as typhus and yellow fever.

At the same time the United States, now secure within its own borders, began to take an interest in foreign affairs. Cuba, only ninety miles off the coast of Florida, would be a convenient place for

American military bases. Also, the island's acres of sugar cane seemed a good possibility for trade.

On the Brink of War

In 1897, President William McKinley, hoping to calm the growing tensions on the island, persuaded the Spanish to grant the Cubans more political rights. But partial freedom only increased the rebels' determination to get rid of the Spanish for good.

Remington predicted war. So did the owner and publisher of the *New York Journal*, William Randolph Hearst. What better way to sell newspapers than to be first on the scene at a war, reasoned Hearst. He hired Remington and a popular reporter named Richard Harding Davis to take a trip to Cuba. There they would make contact with the Cuban rebels' leader, General Máximo Gómez, and get the "scoop" in words and pictures.

Eva Remington worried about her husband sailing straight into a dangerous situation. But Remington was itching to go. He and Davis took a steamship to Havana, Cuba, in early 1897. Remington thought that the mission would be the most exciting one of his career. It turned out to be one of the most boring. He and Davis were unable to reach the rebels, who were hiding in the country-side. Nor did they see any attacks. Instead Remington interviewed General Weyler, made

Yellow Journalism

William Randolph Hearst and his rival Joseph Pulitzer, publisher of the *New York World*, were two of the major creators of "yellow journalism." Their newspapers specialized in reporting sensational and often shocking events. They sold to millions by exposing political corruption, advertising quack medicines, and printing the first "funny papers," or comic strips. Perhaps most successful of all were the papers' emotional stories of scandal and crime—respectable citizens going insane, dead bodies found in alleyways. Whenever possible, these stories were illustrated. And sometimes Hearst and Pulitzer even made up their own "news."

sketches of the island, and waited for something to happen. He cabled his employer, Hearst: "Everything is quiet. . . . There will be no war. I wish to return."[1]

William Randolph Hearst's reply made newspaper history: "Please remain. You furnish the pictures and I'll furnish the war."[2]

After one month Remington returned anyway. He illustrated Davis's new book, *Cuba in Wartime*, and Hearst was pleased. The book helped to stir up war fever in the United States.

At home Remington was waging his private war against food and drink. For exercise he took up the latest craze, bicycling. ("Everyone in America is riding 'bike.' It makes the grease come out of a fellow," Remington once said.[3]) But any progress he made in weight control was soon undone. He loved his pleasures too much. After his customary summer vacation at Cranberry Lake, he wrote to Poultney Bigelow, "I am at 240 lbs. and nothing can stop me but an incurable disease."[4] Remington carried on anyway, painting and writing and planning a trip to Montana to hunt at Buffalo Bill Cody's ranch.

In 1897, in a bid to have his pictures judged on their own merits, instead of as illustrations, he published his first picture book, *Drawings*. It would be followed four years later by *A Bunch of Buckskins*, a book containing just eight colorful pastels. The last and most successful collection of drawings, *Done in the Open*, would appear in 1902, with an introduction, full of praise, by Wister.

"Remember the *Maine*"

By 1898, the situation in Cuba demanded more American attention. President McKinley sent the battleship U.S.S. *Maine* to Havana Harbor to protect United States citizens on the island. On the morning of February 15, the ship suddenly blew up, killing all the sailors on board. The papers of Hearst and Pulitzer blamed the explosion on Spain, although there was no proof at all as to the cause of the catastrophe. The only thing certain was that now the United States would have to fight. Angry shouts of "Remember the *Maine*" were heard in the streets. On April 25, after Spain declared war on the United States, Congress declared war on Spain.

Remington jumped at the chance to be an illustrator/correspondent in the Spanish-American War and hurried to Florida to watch the troops sail for Cuba. Expecting the sketching opportunity of his lifetime, Remington waited impatiently for the fighting to begin.

He was well connected for this war. Theodore Roosevelt had quit his job as assistant secretary of the Navy to help form the First United States Volunteer Cavalry, of which the Rough Riders were a part. (Roosevelt would be promoted to colonel in charge of the soon-to-be-famous group of volunteers.) And Remington's old friend General Nelson Miles was now commanding general of the Army.

The invasion itself was to be headed by General William Shafter. When it finally began, Remington was given special permission to sail ashore on Shafter's command ship, the U.S.S. *Seguranca.* On June 22, fifteen thousand American soldiers landed in Cuba and headed for the city of Santiago, where much of the Spanish army waited. Remington landed too, carrying everything he needed on his back—camera, sketchbook, gun, and

Theodore Roosevelt (center with glasses) and his Rough Riders became famous during the Spanish-American War.

a pack containing crackers, coffee, and a silver flask of whiskey.

War in Cuba

It was hard for a man as heavy as Remington to follow the troops through the jungle in the suffocating heat. He had found a companion, a writer named John Fox. Neither Fox nor Remington had a tent, so they slept in the open, in the mud and rain. When they had eaten their three days' worth of rations, the correspondents had to beg for coffee and crackers from an officer and eat coconuts that they picked from the trees.

As the army pushed toward Santiago, the shooting began. Remington found it nerve-racking that the enemy was invisible in the thick jungle, although the sound of Spanish bullets and shrapnel were all around.

On July 1, General Shafter's army attacked San Juan Hill (and nearby Kettle Hill), which the Spanish had fortified to defend Santiago. Remington did not see the Rough Riders or any other soldiers charging, but he heard their tremendous shout of victory when they reached the hilltop. He climbed San Juan Hill later and came face-to-face with the dead. He wrote of this sight: "Their set teeth shone through their parted lips, and they were horrible."[5] Old friends from the American-Indian-fighting cavalry were there; and Remington saw soldiers running, "some of them shot in the face, bleeding hideously."[6] Fighting continued, but by nightfall the Americans were firmly in control.

The battle was the decisive one in the short war. Santiago fell to the Americans two weeks later, and Spain surrendered on August 12, 1898. Cuba gained its independence. As a result of the Spanish-American War, the United States emerged as a world power, taking from Spain the islands of Guam and

Puerto Rico. The Philippines, as well, were given to the United States in exchange for $20 million.

Immediately after the battle of San Juan Hill, Remington had become ill with the fever that was spreading through the troops, so he returned to New York on a hospital ship. Back home with Eva he was a different man from the one who had longed to see a war. In the Cuban jungle he had seen the real horror of it. Deeply shaken, he left behind forever his boyhood fantasies of noble battle. Perhaps even harder for him to accept was the fact that he was not a hero like his father, only a war correspondent who had dodged bullets like almost everyone else.

Painting the Rough Riders

Depressed, Remington produced very little work on the subject of the Spanish-American War. But his article "With the Fifth Corps," published in *Harper's Monthly*, was powerful. In this starkly realistic account, the author tells how he was haunted by the dead bodies that gleamed white in the moonlight. Trying to describe the scene after the fighting, he is almost at a loss for words: "All the broken spirits, bloody bodies, hopeless, helpless suffering . . . are so much more appalling than anything else in the world."[7]

The two oil paintings he made of the war achieved a life of their own. They are still used today to illustrate articles on Cuba in encyclopedias and history books. *The Scream of Shrapnel at San Juan Hill, Cuba* depicts soldiers under Spanish fire. As in many of Remington's western battle scenes, the enemy is not shown. *Charge of the Rough Riders at San Juan Hill* shows Theodore Roosevelt on horseback, gallantly leading his men to victory. Although Remington never actually witnessed such a scene, the picture made celebrities of the Rough Riders and caused Roosevelt to be hailed as a great hero. Roosevelt went on to win the governorship of New York in 1898. And two years later, in 1900, William McKinley won his second election to the presidency,

In 1898, Frederic Remington depicted one of the most famous battles of the Spanish-American War in Charge of the Rough Riders at San Juan Hill.

with Roosevelt as vice president. The White House is where the influential painting hangs today.

Before they disbanded, the Rough Riders presented Colonel Roosevelt with a cast of Remington's statuette *The Bronco Buster*. This did much to lift the artist's spirits. It was "the greatest compliment I ever had . . .," he told Roosevelt. "After this everything will be mere fuss."[8]

Tough Times

But only work could really pull Remington out of his black mood, although it took him a long time to recover from the experiences of war. He decided to return to his tried-and-true theme—the struggle for the West.

And for the most part, he stuck to it. The oil *Missing*, painted in 1899, is a western desert scene in which a soldier, with hands tied and a rope around his neck, is being led by his American Indian captors to his death. This is the last picture that Remington submitted to the National Academy of Design. When it failed to win him "Academician" status, he washed his hands of the whole institution.

Another blow to his ego came that year. Harper & Brothers were no longer giving him projects. Facing serious financial problems, the publishing company was hiring cheaper, less famous artists and writers. To Remington it was unthinkable that he should be rejected after a fruitful fifteen-year partnership, and he was furious.

Sundown Leflare

Before the Spanish-American War, Remington had branched out from reporting to a more challenging type of writing—fiction. From 1897 to 1902, he would write stories and novels about life from the American Indian point of view. The competition in the field of Western literature was impressive, so Remington took a risk when he entered this new territory. In 1899, his first book of fiction was published. It was a collection of five illustrated stories, which took its title, *Sundown Leflare*, from its main character.

Remington modeled the character after a man named L'Heureux, whom he had known out West. He drew Sundown Leflare to look exactly like a photograph of the real man—stiff black hair, narrow eyes in a strong-boned face, a sombrero in his hand, and a gun on his hip. Sundown was part French, part American Indian.

In the stories, Sundown and the white man often do not see eye to eye. The wide gap between the American Indian and the white man is a theme that Remington would continue to explore. He would soon be drawn even closer to the western subjects that he knew best.

9

NOVELS AND LOST WAX

When Frederic Remington was born, the United States was a land of farms and forests. By 1900, when he was almost forty years old, the country had transformed itself into the world's leading industrial nation. Telephones, electric lights, phonographs, and skyscrapers, all exciting novelties in Remington's youth, were now part of everyday life. The Wright brothers would soon make the first successful airplane flight. And the first gasoline-powered automobiles were already chugging along the country's bumpy roads. But Remington loved horses too much ever to buy a car. Nostalgic for the old days, he wanted very little to do with the noisy new century.

Ingleneuk

For six thousand dollars he and Eva bought the little island of Ingleneuk in the North Country. In Chippewa Bay, it was part of the Thousand Islands chain, which dots the St. Lawrence River. Covered with pine trees and white birch, Ingleneuk had a house and its own tiny beach. The Remingtons also built a boathouse, a tennis court, and a separate art

Frederic Remington stands on the shore of his island, Ingleneuk, as he gets ready for a canoe trip.

studio, which faced Canada and the northern light. Now they would not have to spend their country summers at a hotel.

This quiet place became Remington's favorite escape from "publishers' telephones" and all the "fuss that makes life down in the big clearing."[1] It was not far from Ogdensburg, and it was so peaceful and beautiful that Remington called it his idea of heaven. From 1900 to 1908 he would look forward impatiently to summers at his private hideaway on the river.

Remington arranged his life on Ingleneuk much as he did at Endion, with plenty of time for hard work and outdoor play. He awoke at 6:00 A.M. for a swim in the cold St. Lawrence and was ready an hour later for a huge breakfast of pork chops, fried potatoes, and coffee. He spent most of the day in his studio, but when 3:00 P.M. came, he was like a boy let out of school. Almost every afternoon he took his favorite canoe, the *Nacoochee*, out on the river. (He would buy a motor boat only when he grew too fat to paddle.) In the evenings the Remingtons and visiting friends could sit on the porch and watch the sunset. There were few distractions on the little island. At Ingleneuk Remington worked with great concentration, inspired by the water, the whispering forest, the changing light.

Painting the North Country

Although the world knew Remington as a western artist, some of his most wonderful paintings are North Country scenes. Two such pictures were completed in 1905, when Remington was becoming more confident about his ability to paint color. In *Coming to the Call*, a moose is lured by a hunter's fake moose call. The animal's noble head and antlers are silhouetted against the orange glow of the evening and reflected in the water. The scene is as vivid as a jewel. Many people consider *Evening on a Canadian Lake* to be Remington's greatest painting. In it two woodsmen paddle their canoe at dusk over the still water. Deep blues and shadows and the last rays of the sun create a breathtaking calm. Just as the canoe is reflected in the lake, the painting reflects the artist's reverence for the beauty of nature.

First Novel

During his first summer on the island, Remington wrote his first novel, *The Way of an Indian*, although it would not be published until 1905. It is in keeping with the serious mood that Remington brought home from the Spanish-American War. Like his short stories about Sundown Leflare, it is an effort to see life from the American Indian side, and it shows that the author was thinking differently from ten years before, when he had reported on the events at Wounded Knee.

The Way of an Indian tells the story of a Cheyenne warrior. As a boy he is called White Otter, and he lives with his people near the Rocky Mountains, daydreaming of heroic deeds. When the "Good God" gives him his medicine, or power, he takes the name The Bat. Year after year he watches as the white people intrude on the land. Their "talking wires" (telegraphs) and railroads threaten the buffalo herds, which are as precious as life itself to the Cheyenne.

In a fight with some white hunters, The Bat earns a warrior's name—The Fire Eater. He becomes a great chief and a fighter for his people. But he knows that the endless stream of white settlers can never be stopped: "Many of their scalps shall dry in our lodges, but brother, we cannot kill them all."[2]

The Fire Eater reaches old age only to have his village destroyed by soldiers one bitter cold night. When his son freezes to death in his arms, there is nothing left for the old chief but death, too. He waits for it alone in the snow. Remington writes, "He wanted to go to the spirit land where the Cheyennes of his home and youth were at peace in warm valleys, talking and eating."[3]

First to Use the "Lost-Wax" Method

The most remarkable event of 1900 for Remington was his discovery of a new way to make sculpture. In 1898, the Henry-Bonnard Bronze Company, which had cast all of his statuettes, had burned to the ground. For Remington this turned out to be a blessing in disguise. He switched to Roman Bronze Works, a foundry in Brooklyn owned by Riccardo Bertelli. Instead of sand casting, Bertelli used the "lost-wax" process of creating a bronze. It was a very old technique, but it gave Remington a brilliant new start. It allowed him more freedom to make subtle changes and create fine detail, and he could make each wax cast slightly different from the others. "Just see what can be done with it—isn't it wonderful!" wrote Remington.[4]

Remington was the first American sculptor to use the lost-wax method. It enabled him to become a master of his art and produce unique bronzes— mostly cowboys, soldiers, American Indians, and horses—that were more expressive than ever before. Between 1900 and 1907 he created thirteen statuettes using the new process. And because he was so pleased with the results, he remade some sand-cast pieces in lost wax, too.

Remington's first work cast by Roman Bronze Works is called *The Norther*. It is a sculpture of a horse and rider bracing themselves against the

How a "Lost-Wax" Bronze is Made

In lost-wax casting, workers first make a replica of the clay sculpture out of wax. The artist can then rework the easily shaped surface, "painting on" textures with a brush and making the wax model even more detailed than the original piece of clay.

When the wax model is finally completed, it is placed in a container filled with a liquid substance called the investment. The container is then baked in a kiln, and the investment hardens to form a mold. But in the heat the wax sculpture inside melts, flowing down various escape channels to be "lost."

Workers pour molten bronze into the investment mold. The hot metal forms a shape identical to the wax cast because it fills up the space once occupied by the "lost" material. When cool, the bronze is ready to be polished and colored.

wicked blast of the north wind. Because of the freedom of the lost-wax process, Remington was able to make every detail stand out, down to the hairs on the horse's windblown tail. *The Norther* is as dramatic as *The Bronco Buster* in its own way. No action is shown at all, but the invisible force of the wind gives the piece its power. "Both man and horse almost frozen,"[5] is how the artist described this intense sculpture.

The Norther was quickly followed by more. His next work, *The Cheyenne*, sold very well at Tiffany's, and Remington himself thought that it was so lifelike that it was "burning the air."[6] It captures in bronze one split second as a warrior and his horse fly along at full gallop. In this statuette

Frederic Remington felt The Cheyenne *was one of his most life-like bronzes.*

Remington solved the problem of balance by cleverly using the Cheyenne's buffalo robe as a support.

In 1902 he made *Coming through the Rye*, which is second only to *The Bronco Buster* in popularity. It is a group piece in which four cowboys are riding into town for some fun after a long, dusty cattle drive. Whooping and hollering, they shoot their guns into the air to signal the start of their spree. The statuette was so hard to perfect that Remington wrote to Wister, ". . . day after day I am to do this until I die or complete this bronze."[7] But he did

Coming Through the Rye *remains one of Frederic Remington's most famous bronzes.*

complete it, and a cast of the rowdy cowboys is at the White House today.

The Virginian

While Remington was struggling with his cowboy group, Owen Wister published his classic book, *The Virginian*. It was the first cowboy novel ever written, and it quickly became a best-seller as edition after edition flew out of the bookstores. Readers were charmed by Wister's romantic account of life out West. And the main character, the Virginian, became America's idea of what a cowboy should be. Gentle inside, tough on the outside, he would rather not fight, but he was always prepared: "When you call me that, smile."[8] Countless cowboys would be modeled after Wister's hero, and Remington was jealous.

The two men never worked together after 1902. Remington had promised to do the illustrations for *The Virginian*, but when the time came, he flatly refused, telling Wister he was too busy. And he was.

John Ermine of the Yellowstone

Remington put all the finishing touches on the wax cast of *Coming Through the Rye* and hurried up to Ingleneuk to spend the summer of 1902 writing his own western novel, *John Ermine of the Yellowstone*. It was to be Remington's answer to *The*

Virginian—a story of the real West as he saw it, instead of a romance with a hero who, he thought, seemed too good to be true. All through the summer he sat writing at the cluttered desk in his studio. Writing was much more difficult for him than painting or sculpting, but he pushed himself hard. Finally, by summer's end, he had finished. He paddled his canoe to a friend's island nearby and said joyfully, "I've coined two words to-day—the sweetest ones in the English language. . . ." Then he shouted in his neighbor's ear, "T-H-E E-N-D!"[9]

John Ermine of the Yellowstone is the story of a blonde-haired white man who has been raised by the Crow Indians as one of their own. Called White Weasel as a child, he scampers freely over his prairie home with his friends, playing war games and learning to hunt. When he grows older, he earns the respect of the tribe as a pony herder and comes to understand "all things in nature."[10]

The Crow often sided with the whites against their enemies, the Sioux. So after Custer's defeat in 1876, White Weasel takes the English name of John Ermine and goes to live among the soldiers as a scout. Trustworthy and highly skilled in his new job, Ermine believes that he has been accepted into the white man's world.

But he falls desperately in love with Katherine Searles, the major's flirtatious daughter. When she rejects his proposal of marriage, he is crushed. What is worse, he is badly insulted by the young officer who is Katherine's real fiancé. Ermine realizes with a shock that even though he is white, the soldiers look down on him because they see him as an American Indian. It does not matter that he has often saved their lives in battle with the Sioux and kept them from freezing to death in the snow; ". . . here among the huts and the women I am a dog."[11] In a rage he seeks revenge, only to be shot to death himself.

The book did not sell as well as Wister's *The Virginian*. It had some success, but not enough to satisfy Remington. He was doubly disappointed when a play adapted from the novel flopped in New York. He realized that although his writing was good, his art was better, and he never attempted another book.

Yet Theodore Roosevelt, who had become president of the United States after McKinley's assassination in 1901, admired his friend's fiction and wrote to Remington, ". . . you come closer to the real thing . . ." than almost any other Western author.[12] The story of the doomed hero John Ermine reveals the dark side of Remington's vision—when two cultures meet, the result is often misunderstanding, and sometimes death.

10

THE "REMINGTON NUMBER"

Remington took stock of his whirlwind career as the new century began and concluded, "I have spread myself out too thin."[1] Even though his old mainstay, *Harper's*, had dropped him, his illustrations were appearing in most of the popular magazines of the day—*Century*, *Outing*, *Cosmopolitan*, *Scribner's*, *The Saturday Evening Post*, *Woman's Home Companion*, and *Collier's Weekly*. And this was just the everyday work that he did to pay the bills. He was also sculpting in the lost-wax method, painting, and writing a novel.

A New Century and a New Direction

In 1900 he was awarded an honorary degree from Yale. A celebrity himself, he socialized with other

Frederic Remington painted this self-portrait, called Self-Portrait on a Horse, *in 1901.*

leading citizens—artists and writers, bankers and business people, government officials, and military men of the highest rank. And he was close friends with President Theodore Roosevelt, who invited him to dine at the White House. Fifteen years after riding out of Kansas City on an old mare, Frederic Remington had achieved success far beyond his youthful fantasies. But it was not enough.

One thing had escaped him all these years— fame as a painter. He passionately wanted to leap ahead with oils as he had with sculpture. So in 1902, after completing the novel *John Ermine of the Yellowstone*, he made a momentous decision: Not only would he stop writing fiction, but he would never illustrate again. As hard as it was to give up the secure income from magazine work, Remington would spend the rest of his life pursuing his highest goal—immortality in bronze and paint.

The Fading West

Remington had been going West for several years now in search not of Geronimo but of beautiful color. After his first summer at Ingleneuk, he took the long train ride to the Rocky Mountains of Colorado and on to New Mexico and Mexico. At the Ute Indian reservation and the village of the Pueblo Indians, he sketched people and horses. He also added to his collection of southwestern treasures with cliff-dweller pottery, baskets, weapons, and beaded clothes—"the best stuff you ever saw."[2]

But as the whistling, smoking train puffed its way over the land, Remington saw that "his West" had become quite civilized. The twentieth century had reached even remote corners of the region, and it was far different from the wilderness he had loved as a young man. So many of the old-time characters were gone that Remington would say, "Cowboys! There are no cowboys anymore."[3] He wrote about his disappointment to Eva:

Dear Kid:

. . . Shall never come west again—It is all brick buildings—derby hats and blue overhauls—it spoils my early illusions . . .[4]

But he would come West several times more, to South Dakota, Texas, Wyoming, Montana, and Mexico. The land itself was still the same, with its clear, tumbling rivers and jagged snow-topped mountains. The light was still sharp, the colors still clear. And color was what he had come to study as he sought a new direction for his art.

Never for a minute did he consider giving up his western themes. He just wanted to paint them in a different way. How could he close the gap between his old "action" paintings and the fine art of the day?

It would be a great challenge, especially since he had long been thought of as an action painter. But Remington's ambition was boundless, and he never shrank from a difficult job.

After his upsetting experience in the Spanish-American War, he had lost interest in painting heroic moments in painstaking detail. His new emphasis—on simplicity, mood, and color—was a radical change for Remington: "Big art is a process of elimination, cut down and out—do your hardest work outside the picture, and let your audience take away something to think about—to imagine."[5]

Remington's Nocturnes

Once Remington had told Wister that all scenes must occur in the daylight. In 1899, however, Remington had seen an exhibition of nocturnes, or nighttime scenes, by a California artist named Charles Rollo Peters. Attracted to their mysterious atmosphere, he began to paint nocturnes himself. The muted colors, the gleam of moonlight, the blurred outlines of shapes in the shadows were all hard to capture. At Ingleneuk, Remington paddled out on the river when the moon was high, just to look. Slowly he taught himself to build up tone upon tone of the same color to achieve the desired effect—his first experiments with Tonalism. A "new" Remington emerged.

One of these early nocturnes is the 1901 oil *Old Stage Coach of the Plains*. It is a glimpse of bygone days painted in the artist's latest technique. The Overland Mail coach, which delivered mail throughout the West, is making its way in the dark of night. A spot of light shines through the coach window, and a man with a rifle sits on the roof, for this was American Indian country, and stagecoach travel could be a dangerous thing.

A Reconnaissance is in similar tones of blue, green, and brown. Here an American Indian scout waits silently with the horses while two cavalrymen search for signs of the enemy. An expanse of white snow reflects the moonlight in the cold, starry night.

The new nocturnes were the center of attention when Remington held an exhibit at New York's Clausen Gallery in 1901. Because he showed fifteen oil paintings and ten pastels, he considered this show to be his first as a fine artist, instead of an illustrator. From now on he would complete one amazing painting after another.

Experimentation With Impressionism

Impressionism, as well as Tonalism, now fascinated Remington. At The Players Club he had met members of a group of Impressionist artists known as "The Ten." As Remington studied their use of light and color, his sunlit scenes began to change, too.

Impressionism

Impressionism is a style of painting that began in France, in the 1860s and 1870s. Artists such as Claude Monet, Auguste Renoir, and Edgar Degas dedicated them-selves to depicting scenes of everyday life—people sitting in cafés and parks, playing with their children, attending horse races and ballets—and they painted them in a revolutionary new way. They often used choppy brushstrokes and blurred outlines. Above all, they experimented with the shimmering interplay of light, shadow, and color.

In the late 1880s, Impressionism came to America. The artists who became the country's best-known Impressionists formed a group called "The Ten." Like most of their French counterparts, they loved to paint outside instead of in the studio. Three prominent members of the group were William Merritt Chase, Frank Benson, and Willard Metcalf. Chase is famous for his blue-green scenes of Long Island's beaches and hills. Benson depicted his daughters and son in sparkling sunlight, as they played with the family dog or sat in a rowboat. And Metcalf painted the New England hills, often in winter, as snow fell over the land in what he called a mysterious "white veil."

When he painted *Remington's Boat House at Ingleneuk,* he told an island neighbor, "Got to take some of the light and water home with me to look at this winter."[6] North Country life inspired him to depart from his western scenes and paint landscapes the way The Ten did—in the open air. This little "waterscape" glows like an emerald and shows the short brush strokes and wavy outlines of the Impressionist style. Remington displayed it in 1903 at New York's Noé Gallery in the first of four exhibits he would hold there. *Boat House* surprised critics who expected only cowboys and American Indians from the country's greatest western artist.

Remington's Boat House at Ingleneuk, *painted in 1903, was a break from his normal subject of the American West and was done in an Impressionist style.*

A New Opportunity With *Collier's Weekly*

Much of his best new work was being reproduced in the pages of *Collier's Weekly*, and this more than made up for the gap left by *Harper's*. *Collier's* magazine was growing fast, publishing well-known illustrators like Charles Dana Gibson and famous writers, such as Rudyard Kipling and Sir Arthur Conan Doyle. To Remington's intense satisfaction *Collier's* did not mind that he no longer made pictures to illustrate articles. His paintings appeared in the magazine by themselves, as important double-page spreads and front covers. *Collier's* also began selling individual prints of his works for one dollar apiece. These inexpensive prints made great art available to the vast middle class, and soon Remington's colorful pictures decorated living rooms all over America. *Collier's* art editor, George Wharton Edwards, loved almost everything that Remington produced. He sent the artist funny little poems to encourage him and wrote, "Keep on sending 'em—you're doing better work all the time! I want more—more!"[7]

Then in 1903, *Collier's* offered Remington a dream of a contract. They would pay him one thousand dollars a month for four years in exchange for twelve paintings each year. All of the pictures would be reproduced in color and could be on any subject of his choosing. An income of twelve thousand dollars a year, a very large salary at the time, guaranteed him financial security. And, of course, Remington would make much more money by selling the original oils that he made for *Collier's*.

Harper's had given him his start, but *Collier's* was giving him the chance to be seen solely as a painter. He was free from financial worries and free to paint anything his imagination invented. Remington could now concentrate totally on a painter's problems, such as color, form, brushwork, and mood.

He worked strictly according to schedule. Before each summer he planned and roughly sketched most of the year's twelve paintings. Then, in the peace and quiet of Ingleneuk, he completed them, often at the rate of one a week. For *Collier's*, Remington actually slowed down in order to polish and perfect his paintings. (He used to finish an illustration in a couple of hours.)

The first painting published under the new contract is called *His First Lesson*. Its setting is the exotic San José de Bavicora in Mexico, where ranch hands are breaking in a wild horse. The adobe buildings and yellow earth that Remington saw in his 1893 visit appear in the painting. But the picture's loose brushwork and violet-colored shadows show the Impressionist influence of 1903.

Even more of a departure from the artist's old style is *Fight for the Waterhole*. Working from an old photograph taken in Arizona, Remington created a simplified landscape with few of his usual details. The blues and yellows and browns are softly blended. And the tension in the scene comes not from violent action but because the cowboys are nervously waiting for shooting to break out.

Historical Paintings

While many oils for *Collier's* were single works, Remington also completed three historical series for the magazine. And although the paintings all have stories to tell, they too display the new pared-down background and blended colors. The *Louisiana Purchase* series was the first, published in 1904. It is a history in pictures of how the West was settled, beginning with wandering fur trappers and pioneers heading for the wilderness. It moves on to show wagon trains under attack, stagecoaches struggling through snowdrifts, and Texas cowboys on the cattle trail. In the last picture, *End of the Day*, men and horses work at dusk on a ranch in the already tamed West. Two more series, *The Great Explorers* and *Tragedy of the Trees*, would follow in the years to come.

The *Louisiana Purchase* pictures were shown at the Noé Gallery in 1905. Unlike Remington's previous exhibits, only his newest oils were included, and critics now had a chance to see at close hand the superb work he was doing for *Collier's*. An influential art critic named Royal Cortissoz sent the artist a note of praise, saying that it must be ". . . great sport to be alive and doing work like that, making something beautiful that no one else could make."[8] At long last Remington began to feel appreciated for his painting ability. He thanked Cortissoz: "A good word at times is a lot of comfort."[9]

More Fame and Fortune

Remington's bronzes too received attention in 1905. The Knoedler Gallery, one of New York's most prestigious, mounted a show of nine Remington sculptures. On display was one of the artist's favorites, the just-finished statuette *The Rattlesnake*. It is similar to his first piece, *The Bronco Buster*, only this horse rears frantically in order to avoid a snake that is coiled at its feet. Also, in 1905, the Corcoran Art Gallery in Washington, D.C., bought one cast each of *The Mountain Man* and *Coming Through the Rye*— the first of Remington's sculptures to belong to a museum. Recognition for Remington's paintings and bronze sculptures was growing all the time, and his works in both these fields were becoming quite

expensive. Triumphantly, he wrote, "I hit em for a few this season."[10]

On March 18, 1905, the forty-four-year-old artist was in the limelight again. In an extremely rare gesture, *Collier's* devoted its entire issue just to him. A celebration of his life and art, it was entitled the "Remington Number." There could be no better publicity. The issue included a photograph of Remington standing in front of the fireplace in his Endion studio. It contained photographs of four of his bronzes, and it reproduced in color many of his best paintings. The North Country masterpiece *Evening on a Canadian Lake* was featured as the centerfold. *Collier's* sold individual prints of the paintings in the issue and announced that the origi-

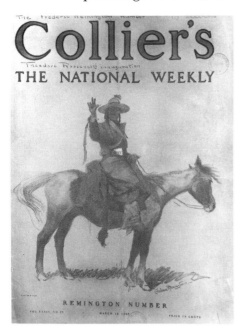

nals were for sale at the Noé Gallery. Throughout the magazine there were tributes by friends, including one in which Owen Wister called Remington "a national treasure."[11]

Collier's *special issue, the "Remington Number," was completely devoted to the works of Frederic Remington.*

But one of the most interesting articles was a short one written by the artist himself, "A Few Words from Mr. Remington." In it he recalls his first trip West in 1881, when he was nineteen years old. It was then, he writes, as he warmed himself by the old wagon freighter's campfire, that he decided to become an artist of the West. Actually, a few more years would pass before the young man would dedicate himself completely to his art, but that first vision of the majestic land stayed with him forever.

He also tells the reader that at first he had not realized what a difficult profession he had chosen. It had always been "more a matter of heart than head,"[12] and his love for his work had always seen him through. The year of the "Remington Number," 1905, America's most famous western artist looked back with nostalgia at the old days. He describes how he felt privileged to have seen the last years of the frontier: "I saw the living, breathing end of three American centuries of smoke and dust and sweat, and I now see quite another thing where it all took place, but it does not appeal to me."[13]

11

"I AM PERFORMING MIRACLES"

fter ten years of sculpting small statues, Remington dreamed of doing a full-sized bronze, or "big mud." In March 1905 he got his chance. The Fairmount Park Art Association asked him to make a statue of a cowboy on a horse to decorate Philadelphia's large municipal park. The Philadelphians had chosen Remington because the year's bronze and painting exhibits and the special issue of *Collier's* had sent his fame sky-high. "I cannot thank you enough," wrote Remington when he accepted the offer.[1] He immediately visited Fairmount Park and chose a rocky hilltop as the best site for his cowboy. Then he rushed home to get to work.

First he made a small clay version of the statue, which the park committee approved in December 1905. A few months later, Remington signed the final contract. He was not offered a great deal of money for the project, but he did not seem to mind. It was accomplishment, not money, that he was after. As he wrote to Professor Leslie Miller, secretary of the committee, ". . . I intend to give you people a piece of horse-bronze which will sit up in any company. You can bet a few on that, Prof."[2]

The next stage was the creation of a four-foot-high "working model." By early 1907, Remington finished that, too. The park committee visited his

Remington's Fellow Sculptors

There were many fine American sculptors working during Remington's lifetime. One of the most celebrated was Augustus Saint-Gaudens, who specialized in very large statues. His *Shaw Memorial*, in Boston, commemorates an African-American commander in the Civil War. Saint-Gaudens's bronzes of Abraham Lincoln and many other famous Americans can be found in public parks.

The work of Daniel French is perhaps even better known to present-day Americans, because he is the artist who sculpted the Lincoln Memorial in Washington, D.C.

studio to see it, since it would be identical to the completed monument. But one stuffy, demanding member objected to the stiff, outstretched front leg of the horse. It *was* an unusual pose for a horse-themed statue, but it was realistic, the artist argued. "I am trying to give you a Remington broncho and am not following the well-known receipt [recipe] for making a horse," he explained.[3] And he refused to change it.

At last, by the end of 1907, he was ready to make the "big mud." He built a special studio for the job. It had a turntable platform and a sliding track that led outside, so that when weather permitted he could model in the natural light, something no American sculptor had ever done before.

Day after day he worked perched on a ladder, since the cowboy's head would be more than fourteen feet from the ground. When the huge clay model was finally ready for inspection, the artist wrote gleefully to Leslie Miller, "It's a dandy, Professor, and I am not a bit afraid of your old committee—."[4] After the Philadelphians gave their approval, Bertelli's foundry made the wax cast. Remington perfected that, then tinkered with the final bronze version of the statue, and his job was done.

The Cowboy, reining in his horse on the rocky ledge in Fairmount Park, is an authentic Texas cowboy from the days of the cattle boom, one of

Remington's beloved "Plainsmen who traveled by the stars."[5] The statue was installed in June 1908. During the formal installation ceremony, a group of American Indians and cowboys posed near the bronze, and flowery speeches were made. "I feel more strongly than ever that it is a magnificent thing," Leslie Miller told the artist.[6] And Remington, who badly wanted to make more statues, answered, "I hope now some one will let me do an indian and a Plains cavalryman and then I will be ready for Glory."[7]

More Critical Acclaim

During the three years spent on *The Cowboy*, Remington did not neglect his painting. *Collier's*

The Cowboy *sits on its rocky ledge in Fairmont Park, Philadelphia.*

was buying so many of the new pictures that it would take years to publish them all. The artist was his own sternest critic, however. In spite of recent masterpieces, he thought he had a long way to go: ". . . for ten years I've been trying to get color in my things and I still don't get it. Why why why can't I get it."[8]

But he did get it. In the next few years, he would paint the most marvelous oils of his life and receive all the praise he had ever wanted.

The Knoedler Gallery, where the most famous artists exhibited, began to give Remington a show every December. His friend the Impressionist painter Childe Hassam called the pictures in the 1906 exhibit ". . . *all* the best things . . ."[9] and they sold for record prices. The painting *Against the Sunset* showed critics how astonishingly far Remington had come since the days when they had called him "just an illustrator." In this western nocturne a cowboy gallops over the darkening sagebrush, while the sunset behind him creates a mood of intense nostalgia. The canvas expresses Remington's feeling about the Old West: "My West passed utterly out of existence so long ago as to make it merely a dream."[10]

Profits from the 1907 Knoedler show were low because of a recent stock market crash, but the exhibit featured the thrilling *Downing the Nigh*

Leader. It is a furious chase scene in which American Indians try to stop the Overland Mail coach by killing its lead horse. The picture is bursting with the kind of Old West action found in the 1889 picture *A Dash for the Timber*, but it is painted with Remington's new, looser style.

The same exhibit included the oil *Fired On*, which depicts the special terror of a night attack by an unseen enemy. This eerie, greenish nocturne was acquired by the National Gallery of Art in Washington, D.C., Remington's first painting to become part of a museum collection.

Now that he felt he was finally on the right track, much of his old work embarrassed him: ". . . my early enemies come to haunt me. . . . I would buy them all if I were able and burn them up."[11] He meant it. At least twice, between 1907 and 1909, Remington built giant bonfires in his backyard and calmly tossed in dozens of paintings that he considered failures. He was determined not to let the old story-telling canvases ruin his hard-won reputation as a fine artist.

Rediscovering Nature

Nature was ever more mysterious to Remington in his middle age. Morning and evening in the winter, he loved to take long walks, sketching landscapes with no figures in them at all. He admired the way a blue river flowed through a field of snow and the way a sunset colored the January sky. And in the summertime at Ingleneuk, the moon over the water was a constant source of wonder. "I have *now* discovered for the first time how to do the *silver sheen* of moonlight," he wrote in 1908.[12]

With a friend that fall, Remington revisited Wyoming and Montana, the country of the Sioux wars. Only forty-seven, he was too heavy to enjoy the trip. On the plains he suffered from the heat, and in the mountains the high altitude bothered him. Hiking was out of the question for a three hundred-pound man. And although he made light of his discomfort in a letter to Eva—"Such is the life of an artist in search of the beautiful"[13]—this would really be his last trip West.

The Knoedler Exhibit of 1908

In 1908, with *The Cowboy* statue finished, Remington had submitted more paintings than usual to the Knoedler Exhibit. And they were among his very best. Critics who had been slow to realize that he was a fine painter now admitted that he belonged to the ranks of the great. For the first time at Knoedler, he showed landscapes, small North Country scenes. And, in his Westerns, it was as if color and light had freed him to express more powerful emotion than ever before.

Most of the pictures were pure nocturnes, but the painting *With the Eye of the Mind* is set in the early evening, while part of the earth is in shadow and part is still light. Three Plains Indians, whose fate is symbolized by the dying day, are staring at the sky. A cloud shaped like a warrior on horseback seems to them a sign from the spirit world.

In his diary Remington wrote about the exhibit of 1908, ". . . it was a triumph. I have landed among the painters."[14]

"The Uncertain Career of a Painter"

By the end of the year, the contract with *Collier's* had expired. There was a new editor now who chose not to renew it because he preferred a different style of art. Also the magazine had an oversupply of Remington works, enough to last several years. The break with *Collier's* did not upset Remington; he did not need their support anymore. On the first day of 1909, he wrote, full of hope, "Here we go again . . . embarked on the uncertain career of a painter."[15]

Besides preparing for the next exhibit at Knoedler's, Remington was busy with the tedious job of packing up his studio at Endion. He and Eva had bought land in Ridgefield, Connecticut, near a small community of Impressionist painters. On the land they had built a mansion that Remington proudly called, "the finest building what ever was."[16] He sold Endion and was also forced to sell Ingleneuk in order to pay for the elaborate construction.

Moving day was May 1. Their new home, Lorul Place, was a "gentleman's farm," surrounded by fields and home to a noisy bunch of cows, pigs, and chickens. In the big barn were Remington's horses, which he kept for riding and pulling wagons. The house and gardens and outbuildings were so grand that the locals began to call the place "Remington Village."[17] Friends came often to visit.

Remington soon got back to work. Moving back and forth between painting and sculpture, he began

Lorul Place was the Remington's home in Ridgefield, Connecticut.

the ambitious statuette *The Stampede*, which would portray in bronze the terrifying event he had already put on canvas. Remington was well satisfied with the recognition his sculptures had received. The Metropolitan Museum in New York now owned *The Bronco Buster, The Cheyenne*, and two other pieces. And because of the success of *The Cowboy* in Fairmount Park, he hoped to do another statue. With that in mind Bertelli began to make a larger version of *The Bronco Buster.*

The Knoedler Exhibit of 1909

"I am performing miracles," wrote Remington joyfully that summer at Lorul Place.[18] The main event of the year would be the Knoedler exhibit, and when it opened on December 4, 1909, he had twenty-three paintings to show. As successful as he was, he was still nervous about how the hard-to-please critics, or "insects of the art columns,"[19] would react.

They gave him even higher praise than the year before: "No American artist interests the people more than Remington does, and none is really better worth going to see."[20] What the crowds who came to Knoedler's saw was Remington's painting at its most extraordinary—full of power and mystery and emotion.

The Winter Campaign is a nocturne in which soldiers and horses huddle around little campfires in a dark, snowy forest. The yellow flames, however, are not enough to ward off the blackness that encloses them. There is a quiet force to this picture.

The Buffalo Runners: Big Horn Basin takes place in the clear Western daylight. A group of American Indians comes tearing up over a rise on a buffalo chase. Remington's dashing brush strokes help to give the impression of breakneck speed. The expanse of prairie and big sky emphasizes the freedom that the buffalo runners once had.

Childe Hassam loved *The Outlier* best of all. This painting, with its harmony of blues, took so unusually long for Remington to finish that he called it "my old companion."[21] The American Indian in the picture has separated from his people and keeps solitary watch on his horse. As in other Remington works, the setting sun symbolizes the end of the Plains Indians' era. *The Outlier* is dramatic in its very stillness. It weaves a haunting spell, like a memory or a dream.

The End to a Short Life

What happiness Remington must have felt now that he was accomplishing what he had set out to do. It seemed that each day brought new discoveries. "I have lots to be thankful for this year," he wrote.[22] But on December 20, as he was preparing for the next year's show, he felt sharp stomach pains, which he thought were caused by a pulled muscle. A fever developed, which he could not shake. He tried to paint anyway, but by December 22 he gave up and went to bed.

Doctors visited and urged an emergency operation. "Cut her loose, Doc," was Remington's brave reply.[23] There, on the kitchen table at Lorul Place, the surgeon found what he had suspected—the patient's appendix had ruptured and infection had spread throughout his body. In those days before antibiotics, Remington was doomed.

He was alert enough on Christmas morning to talk to Eva and open his presents, but later, as a snowstorm swirled outside, he went into a coma. On the hushed, white morning of December 26, 1909, at the height of his artistic powers and only forty-eight years old, Frederic Remington died.

His funeral was held in Canton, New York, in the church where his grandfather had once been pastor. And as Remington had planned, he was buried near his father, Seth, who had been his first hero.

Witness to a Vanishing World

Remington had once told a friend that he wanted his epitaph to read *He Knew the Horse*.[24] These words were never carved on his gravestone, but they did not need to be. His knowledge and love of the horse—and of all the diverse characters who roamed the frontier—shines out from his extraordinary life's work. His passion for his subjects made his life itself a great adventure, as he explored the West in a race with time to see it all. A true original, Remington listened only to his own advice and succeeded on his own terms.

Like the horseman in *The Outlier*, he was a witness to a vanishing world. In image after image he recorded the history of the American West in all its romance and fury. In all his many ways—as reporter and illustrator, as novelist, sculptor, and painter—he preserved our past so that we might always know it. As Theodore Roosevelt wrote: "The soldier, the cowboy and rancher, the Indian, the horses and the cattle of the plains, will live in his pictures and bronzes, I verily believe, for all time."[25]

CHRONOLOGY

1861—Born in Canton, New York, on October 4.

1873—Moves to Ogdensburg, New York; Begins riding and sketching horses.

1875—Is sent to military school in Vermont.

1876—Begins studying at Highland Military School in Massachusetts; Begins drawing soldiers and Western subjects.

1878—Enrolls at Yale's School of Fine Arts.

1879—First drawing is published.

1880—Father dies on February 18.

1881—Takes first trip to the West; Sends first sketch to *Harper's Weekly*, which is later published.

1884—Marries Eva Caten on October 1.

1885—Meets with Henry Harper and publishes drawings from a trip to Arizona in *Harper's Weekly*.

1886—Enrolls in Art Students League; Covers Geronimo's escape in Arizona; Meets Powhatan Clarke; Has twenty-five illustrations published.

1887—Makes many sketches and two oil paintings of the Crow and Blackfoot people in North Dakota and Wyoming; Hired to illustrate Theodore Roosevelt's book *Ranch Life and the Hunting Trail*.

1888—Wins the Hallgarten Prize for *Return of the Blackfoot War Party*; Cuts off communication with his mother after she remarries; Visits Powhatan Clarke, the San Carlos Reservation in Arizona, and Indian Territory (in present-day Oklahoma).

1889—Begins making about five hundred illustrations for new edition of Henry Wadsworth

Longfellow's poem "Hiawatha;" Wins silver medal at the Paris International Exposition; Paints *A Dash for the Timber.*

1890—Publishes 173 illustrations in *Harper's Weekly, Harper's Monthly,* and *Century Magazine;* Paints *The Scout: Friends or Enemies* and *A Cavalryman's Breakfast on the Plains.*

1891—Reports on the December 29, 1890, battle at Wounded Knee Creek; Becomes associate member of the National Academy of Design.

1893—Powhatan Clarke drowns on July 21; Remington meets and collaborates with writer Owen Wister.

1895—Wister's "The Evolution of a Cowpuncher" is published, with five illustrations by Remington; Remington finishes his first sculpture *The Bronco Buster;* His first book, *Pony Tracks,* is published.

1896—Finishes the bronze *The Wounded Bunkie.*

1897—Paints *Through the Smoke Sprang the Daring Soldier;* Hired by William Randolph Hearst to cover growing tensions between Cuba and the United States; Illustrates Richard Harding Davis's book *Cuba in Wartime; Drawings* is published.

1898—Covers the Spanish-American War, which inspires *The Scream of Shrapnel at San Juan Hill, Cuba* and *Charge of the Rough Riders at San Juan Hill;* Finishes two bronzes: *The Wicked Pony* and *The Scalp; Crooked Trails* published.

1899—Paints *Missing; Sundown LeFlare* published; Begins painting nocturnes.

1900—Sculpts thirteen statuettes using the "lost-wax"
–1907 method.

1900—*Men with the Bark On* published; Writes *The Way of the Indian;* Awarded an honorary degree from Yale.

1901—*A Bunch of Buckskins* published; Paints *Old Stage Coach of the Plains*.

1902—*Done in the Open* published; Sculpts *Coming Through the Rye*; Writes *John Ermine of the Yellowstone*.

1903—Exhibits *Remington's Boat House at Ingleneuk*; Signs four-year contract with *Collier's Weekly*; Paints *His First Lesson* and *Fight for the Waterhole*.

1904—*The Louisiana Purchase* series of paintings is published in *Collier's Weekly*.

1905—Has annual exhibits at the Knoedler Gallery in
–1909 New York that include the paintings: *Against the Sunset, Downing the Nigh Leader, Fired On, With the Eye of the Mind, The Winter Campaign, The Buffalo Runners: Big Horn Basin*, and *The Outlier*.

1905—Paints *Coming to Call* and *Evening on a Canadian Lake*; *The Way of the Indian* published; Finishes sculpture *The Rattlesnake*; *Collier's Weekly* publishes entire issue devoted to Remington.

1908—Finishes statue *The Cowboy* for Fairmount Park in Philadelphia, Pennsylvania.

1909—Dies on December 26, at the age of forty-eight.

CHAPTER NOTES

Chapter 1. Recording the American West

1. Allen P. and Marilyn D. Splete, eds., *Frederic Remington: Selected Letters* (New York: Abbeville Press, 1987), p. 14.

2. Stephen E. Ambrose, *Crazy Horse and Custer* (New York: New American Library, 1986), p. 443.

3. Harold and Peggy Samuels, eds., *The Collected Writings of Frederick Remington* (Garden City, N.Y.: Doubleday, 1979), p. 551.

Chapter 2. A Boy From the North Country

1. Atwood Manley, *Some of Frederick Remington's North Country Associations* (Ogdensburg, N.Y.: Northern New York Publishing Company, 1961), p. 11.

2. Allen P. and Marilyn D. Splete, eds., *Frederic Remington: Selected Letters* (New York: Abbeville Press, 1987), p. 17.

3. Ibid., pp. 14–15.

4. Ibid., pp. 21–22.

5. James K. Ballinger, *Frederick Remington* (New York: Abrams, 1989), p. 21.

6. Michael Edward Shapiro and Peter H. Hassrick, *Frederic Remington: The Masterworks* (New York: Abrams, 1988), p. 16.

7. Harold and Peggy Samuels, *Frederic Remington: A Biography* (Garden City, N.Y.: Doubleday, 1982), p. 27.

8. Splete and Splete, p. 23.

9. Samuels and Samuels, p. 28.

10. Robert M. Utley, *The Indian Frontier of the American West, 1846–1890* (Albuquerque: University of New Mexico Press, 1984), p. 189.

11. Harold and Peggy Samuels, eds., *The Collected Writings of Frederick Remington* (Garden City, N.Y.: Doubleday, 1979), p. 551.

12. Shapiro and Hassrick, p. 21.

13. Peter Hassrick, *Frederic Remington* (New York: Abrams, 1973), p. 39.

Chapter 3. "Western Dreams"

1. Harold and Peggy Samuels, eds., *The Collected Writings of Frederick Remington* (Garden City, N.Y.: Doubleday, 1979), pp. 3–4.

2. Atwood Manley, *Some of Frederick Remington's North Country Associations* (Ogdensburg, N.Y.: Northern New York Publishing Company, 1961), p. 23.

3. Allen P. and Marilyn D. Splete, eds., *Frederic Remington: Selected Letters* (New York: Abbeville Press, 1987), p. 33.

4. Harold and Peggy Samuels, *Frederic Remington: A Biography* (Garden City, N.Y.: Doubleday, 1982), p. 51.

5. Ibid., p. 58.

6. Ibid., p. 57.

7. Dee Brown, *Bury My Heart at Wounded Knee* (New York: Holt, 1971), p. 123.

8. Ibid., p. 408.

9. Harold McCracken, *Frederic Remington: Artist of the Old West* (Philadelphia: Lippincott, 1947), p. 48.

10. Ibid.

11. Samuels and Samuels, *Frederic Remington: A Biography*, p. 67.

Chapter 4. Artist of the West

1. Allen P. and Marilyn D. Splete, eds., *Frederic Remington: Selected Letters* (New York: Abbeville Press, 1987), p. 103.

2. James K. Ballinger, *Frederick Remington* (New York: Abrams, 1989), p. 32.

3. Peter Hassrick, *Frederic Remington* (New York: Abrams, 1973), p. 30.

4. Dee Brown, *Bury My Heart at Wounded Knee* (New York: Holt, 1971), p. 410.

5. Harold McCracken, *Frederic Remington: Artist of the Old West* (Philadelphia: Lippincott, 1947), p. 52.

6. Harold and Peggy Samuels, *Frederic Remington: A Biography* (Garden City, N.Y.: Doubleday, 1982), p. 127.

7. Hassrick, p. 31.

8. Samuels and Samuels, p. 96.

9. Splete and Splete, p. 47.

10. Ibid., p. 60.

11. Harold McCracken, ed., *Frederic Remington's Own West* (New York: Dial Press, 1960), p. 74.

12. Ibid., p. 76.

13. Ibid., p. 29.

14. Ibid., p. 33.

15. Atwood Manley, *Some of Frederick Remington's North Country Associations* (Ogdensburg, N.Y.: Northern New York Publishing Company, 1961), p. 40.

16. Hassrick, p. 68.

17. Samuels and Samuels, p. 127.

Chapter 5. The End of the Frontier

1. Allen P. and Marilyn D. Splete, eds., *Frederic Remington: Selected Letters* (New York: Abbeville Press, 1987), p. 75.

2. Harold and Peggy Samuels, *Frederic Remington: A Biography* (Garden City, N.Y.: Doubleday, 1982), p. 131.

3. Michael Edward Shapiro and Peter H. Hassrick, *Frederic Remington: The Masterworks* (New York: Abrams, 1988), p. 22.

4. Ibid., p. 21.

5. Splete and Splete, p. 83.

6. James K. Ballinger, *Frederick Remington* (New York: Abrams, 1989), p. 65.

7. Ibid., p. 182.

8. John C. Ewers, *Artists of the Old West* (Garden City, N.Y.: Doubleday, 1973), p. 216.

9. Ibid.

10. Robert M. Utley, *The Indian Frontier of the American West, 1846–1890* (Albuquerque: University of New Mexico Press, 1984), p. 256.

11. Dee Brown, *Bury My Heart at Wounded Knee* (New York: Holt, 1971), p. 446.

12. Harold and Peggy Samuels, eds., *The Collected Writings of Frederick Remington* (Garden City, N.Y.: Doubleday, 1979), p. 62.

13. Harold McCracken, ed., *Frederic Remington's Own West* (New York: Dial Press, 1960), pp. 253–254.

14. Splete and Splete, p. 129.

15. Ballinger, p. 65.

16. Shapiro and Hassrick, p. 39.

17. Ibid., pp. 22–23.

18. Atwood Manley, *Some of Frederick Remington's North Country Associations* (Ogdensburg, N.Y.: Northern New York Publishing Company, 1961), p. 41.

19. Splete and Splete, p. 162.

20. Shapiro and Hassrick, p. 58.

21. Splete and Splete, p. 82.

Chapter 6. Cowboys

1. Allen P. and Marilyn D. Splete, eds., *Frederic Remington: Selected Letters* (New York: Abbeville Press, 1987), p. 157.

2. Harold McCracken, ed., *Frederic Remington's Own West* (New York: Dial Press, 1960), p. 137.

3. Ibid., p. 145.

4. Splete and Splete, p. 177.

5. Ibid., p. 99.

6. Atwood Manley, *Some of Frederick Remington's North Country Associations* (Ogdensburg, N.Y.: Northern New York Publishing Company, 1961), p. 37.

7. Splete and Splete, p. 238.

8. Harold and Peggy Samuels, *Frederic Remington: A Biography* (Garden City, N.Y.: Doubleday, 1982), p. 195.

9. Ibid., p. 204.

10. Splete and Splete, p. 248.

11. Samuels and Samuels, p. 209.

12. Michael Edward Shapiro and Peter H. Hassrick, *Frederic Remington: The Masterworks* (New York: Abrams, 1988), p. 24.

13. Ibid., p. 21.

14. Samuels and Samuels, p. 209.

15. Rick Stewart, *Frederic Remington: Masterpieces from the Amon Carter Museum* (Fort Worth, Tex.: Amon Carter Museum of Western Art, 1992), p. 22.

16. McCracken, p. 90.

17. Splete and Splete, p. 221.

Chapter 7. "I Am to Endure in Bronze"

1. Peter Hassrick, *Frederic Remington* (New York: Abrams, 1973), p. 36.

2. Harold McCracken, *Frederic Remington: Artist of the Old West* (Philadelphia: Lippincott, 1947), p. 92.

3. Harold and Peggy Samuels, *Frederic Remington: A Biography* (Garden City, N.Y.: Doubleday, 1982), p. 222.

4. Hassrick, p. 37.

5. Samuels and Samuels, p. 224.

6. Brian W. Dippie, *Remington & Russell* (Austin: University of Texas Press, 1994), p. 5.

7. Allen P. and Marilyn D. Splete, eds., *Frederic Remington: Selected Letters* (New York: Abbeville Press, 1987), p. 275.

8. McCracken, p. 89.

9. John Stewart, *Frederic Remington, Artist of the Western Frontier* (New York: Lothrop, Lee, & Shepard, 1971), p. 104.

10. Dippie, p. 60.

11. James K. Ballinger, *Frederick Remington* (New York: Abrams, 1989), p. 90.

12. Dee Brown, *Bury My Heart at Wounded Knee* (New York: Holt, 1971), p. 332.

13. Rick Stewart, Frederic *Remington: Masterpieces from the Amon Carter Museum* (Fort Worth, Tex.: Amon Carter Museum of Western Art, 1992), p. 28.

14. Splete and Splete, p. 204.

Chapter 8. War in Cuba

1. Michael Edward Shapiro and Peter H. Hassrick, *Frederic Remington: The Masterworks* (New York: Abrams, 1988), p. 29.

2. J. C. Furnas, *The Americans: A Social History of the United States 1587–1914* (New York: G.P. Putnam's Sons, 1969), p. 863.

3. Atwood Manley, *Some of Frederick Remington's North Country Associations* (Ogdensburg, N.Y.: Northern New York Publishing Company, 1961), p. 28.

4. Allen P. and Marilyn D. Splete, eds., *Frederic Remington, Selected Letters* (New York: Abbeville Press, 1987), p. 285.

5. Harold and Peggy Samuels, eds., *The Collected Writings of Frederick Remington* (Garden City, N.Y.: Doubleday, 1979), p. 347.

6. Ibid.

7. Ibid., p. 348.

8. Rick Stewart, *Frederic Remington: Masterpieces from the Amon Carter Museum* (Fort Worth, Tex.: Amon Carter Museum of Western Art, 1992), p. 30.

Chapter 9. Novels and Lost Wax

1. Michael Edward Shapiro and Peter H. Hassrick, *Frederic Remington: The Masterworks* (New York: Abrams, 1988), p. 32.

2. Harold and Peggy Samuels, eds., *The Collected Writings of Frederick Remington* (Garden City, N.Y.: Doubleday, 1979), p. 587.

3. Ibid., p. 596.

4. Rick Stewart, *Frederic Remington: Masterpieces from the Amon Carter Museum* (Fort Worth, Tex.: Amon Carter Museum of Western Art, 1992), p. 32.

5. Allen P. and Marilyn D. Splete, eds., *Frederic Remington: Selected Letters* (New York: Abbeville Press, 1987), p. 312.

6. Stewart, p. 34.

7. Peter Hassrick, *Frederic Remington* (New York: Abrams, 1973), p. 42.

8. Owen Wister, *The Virginian* (New York: The Macmillan Company, 1928), p. 7.

9. Harold McCracken, *Frederic Remington: Artist of the Old West* (Philadelphia: Lippincott, 1947), p. 110.

10. Samuels and Samuels, p. 465.

11. Ibid., p. 537.

12. Shapiro and Hassrick, p. 24.

Chapter 10. The "Remington Number"

1. Michael Edward Shapiro and Peter H. Hassrick, *Frederic Remington: The Masterworks* (New York: Abrams, 1988), p. 32.

2. Allen P. and Marilyn D. Splete, eds., *Frederic Remington: Selected Letters* (New York: Abbeville Press, 1987), p. 317.

3. Shapiro and Hassrick, p. 35.

4. Splete and Splete, p. 318.

5. Peter Hassrick, *Frederic Remington* (New York: Abrams, 1973), p. 47.

6. Harold McCracken, *Frederic Remington: Artist of the Old West* (Philadelphia: Lippincott, 1947), p. 110.

7. Splete and Splete, p. 333.

8. James K. Ballinger, *Frederick Remington* (New York: Abrams, 1989), p. 118.

9. Ibid.

10. Splete and Splete, p. 356.

11. Harold and Peggy Samuels, *Frederic Remington: A Biography* (Garden City, N.Y.: Doubleday, 1982), p. 324.

12. Harold and Peggy Samuels, eds., *The Collected Writings of Frederick Remington* (Garden City, N.Y.: Doubleday, 1979), p. 551.

13. Ibid.

Chapter 11. "I Am Performing Miracles"

1. Allen P. and Marilyn D. Splete, eds., *Frederic Remington: Selected Letters* (New York: Abbeville Press, 1987), p. 368.

2. Ibid., p. 377.

3. Michael Edward Shapiro and Peter H. Hassrick, *Frederic Remington: The Masterworks* (New York: Abrams, 1988), p. 223.

4. Splete and Splete, p. 382.

5. Shapiro and Hassrick, p. 227.

6. Splete and Splete, p. 392.

7. Ibid.

8. Rick Stewart, Frederic *Remington: Masterpieces from the Amon Carter Museum* (Fort Worth, Tex.: Amon Carter Museum of Western Art, 1992), p. 42.

9. James K. Ballinger, *Frederick Remington* (New York: Abrams, 1989), p. 128.

10. Harold McCracken, *Frederic Remington: Artist of the Old West* (Philadelphia: Lippincott, 1947), p. 105.

11. Harold and Peggy Samuels, *Frederic Remington: A Biography* (Garden City, N.Y.: Doubleday, 1982), p. 418.

12. Ballinger, p. 138.

13. Splete and Splete, p. 400.

14. Samuels and Samuels, p. 418.

15. Shapiro and Hassrick, p. 37.

16. Splete and Splete, p. 442.

17. McCracken, p. 119.

18. Shapiro and Hassrick, p. 37.

19. Ballinger, p. 142.

20. Ibid.

21. Ibid.

22. Shapiro and Hassrick, p. 67.

23. McCracken, p. 121.

24. Peter Hassrick, *Frederic Remington* (New York: Abrams, 1973), p. 28.

25. Stewart, p. 5.

GLOSSARY

adobe—A brick made of earth or clay and straw and dried.

cavalry—Troops mounted on horseback.

exposure—The time needed to make an image on a photographic plate.

Ghost Dance—A ritual performed by American Indians to prepare for the return of the buffalo and the rebirth of the dead.

Impressionism—A theory or practice in painting where artists favor soft, blurry outlines with choppy brushstrokes to show the effects of light and color.

kiln—A furnace or oven in which something (such as pottery) is hardened, burned, or dried.

lariat—A rope used to catch runaway cattle.

nocturne—A work of art dealing with night.

reservation—An area set aside by the government to be the permanent home to a group of American Indians.

rustler—A cow thief.

scout–A skilled frontiersman who serves as a lookout, reads tracks, finds trails, and locates game.

Tonalism—A theory or practice in painting where artists try to achieve an effect through color harmonization rather than by contrasts.

tone—A shade of color.

vaquero—Spanish for cowboy.

yellow journalism—A type of reporting that uses exaggerations, fabrications, splashy headlines and lavish illustrations to influence its readers.

FURTHER READING

Hirschfelder, Arlene B. *Photo Odyssey: Solomon Carvalho's Remarkable Western Adventure, 1853–54.* New York: Houghton Mifflin Company, 2000.

Marrin, Albert. *Sitting Bull and His World.* New York: Penguin Putnam Books for Young Readers, 2000.

Somerlott, Robert. *The Spanish-American War: "Remember the* Maine*!"* Berkeley Heights, N.J.: Enslow Publishers, Inc., 2002.

Van Steenwyk, Elizabeth. *Frederic Remington.* Danbury, Conn.: Franklin Watts, 1994.

Wittmann, Kelly. *Explorers of the American West.* Broomhall, Pa.: Mason Crest Publishers, 2002.

Woog, Adam. *Daily Life of a Cowboy in the Old West.* Farmington Hills, Mich.: Gale Group, 2002.

INTERNET ADDRESSES

Educational Broadcasting Corporation. "Frederic Remington." *American Masters Online.* © 2001. <http://www.pbs.org/wnet/americanmasters/database/remington_f.html>.

Frederic Remington Art Museum. "Frederic Remington." n.d. <http://www.fredericremington.org/frederic.html>.

ThinkQuest Inc. "Frederic Remington (1861–1909)." *Art and the Influence of War.* © 1995–2002. <http://library.thinkquest.org/C005707F/remington.htm>.

INDEX

Greely H.S. Library
Main St
Cumberland, ME 04021